# A Brain Tumor Changes Everything

# A Brain Tumor Changes Everything

Searching for the Shape of Mercy in a Suffering Season

*A Mother's Memoir*

Jan Woltmann

RESOURCE *Publications* · Eugene, Oregon

A BRAIN TUMOR CHANGES EVERYTHING
Searching for the Shape of Mercy in a Suffering Season: A Mother's Memoir

From Eerdmans for epigraph/poem (Chapter 13) titled "Getting Inside the Miracle" by Luci Shaw (see PDF attached)
From Counterpoint for epigraph/poem (Chapter 16) titled "The Peace of Wild Things" by Wendell Berry (see PDF attached)
New Revised Standard Version Bible, copyright 1989, Division of Christian Education of the National Council of the Churches of Christ in the United States of America. Used by permission. All rights reserved.
Disclaimer: This is a true story, though some names and details have been changed.

Resource Publications
An Imprint of Wipf and Stock Publishers
199 W. 8th Ave., Suite 3
Eugene, OR 97401

www.wipfandstock.com

PAPERBACK ISBN: 978-1-7252-8749-5
HARDCOVER ISBN: 978-1-7252-8751-8
EBOOK ISBN: 978-1-7252-8752-5

02/19/21

Dedicated to my grandchildren:
James, Maya, Adeline, Levi, Emily . . .
and to the generations yet to come.
*May this story live its legend in your bones.*

And how blessed all those in whom you live,
whose lives become roads you travel.

—Psalm 84:5, *The Message*

# Contents

# Acknowledgments

THE WRITING OF THIS memoir was mostly a hidden endeavor, a pursuit done in the corners of my life, while working a job, starting a spiritual direction practice, helping with grandbabies (a pleasurable top priority), and caring for my mom and family. The manuscript was written over the course of three-plus years, beginning in 2016.

Special thanks to Laura Kalmar, my dedicated editor, who believed in this project from its inception, and who stayed with me through all the developmental stages of the writing process, including the time my book felt like a wily teenager. Laura's keen eye for the reader, competent literary skills, and pastoral presence helped shape this manuscript, while her genuine love for this story made it sacred work.

Love and gratitude to my liminal community—to Mary and Gary Reimer and the saints at Imago Dei Winnipeg, to Cheryl Klassen, Sandy Froese, Jeannette Thiessen, Deb Peters, Kym Lukin, and David Butler—my first (after-family) round of readers and tireless cheerleaders. The sheer force of your witness and your travail with me is gift.

Thank you to the Woltmann and Martens families—brothers and sisters, nieces and nephews who continue to voyage with us through thick and thin, in sickness and health. We are beyond lucky to have your unwavering support. And to the cloud of witnesses above, my dad Menno, my mom Annabelle, Norm's mom Irma, and our friend, Warren—the veil is thin and I feel your smiles.

But the biggest gratitudes are saved for last. To my children, Laura and Jeff Mathew, Kate and Nathan Regier, Nate and Diana Woltmann—for loving each other well, and for being a fountain of encouragement. Nate, thanks for letting me tell your wondrous, whirlwind, stubborn story, and for being courageous enough to release its spirit into the world.

And finally, to Norm, my husband of almost forty years, who inspires me daily—you are my sweet and steady man, faithful husband and friend, always believing the best about me. Our lives are lived on a holy threshold. I love you forever.

# Prologue

"WHY DID YOU GET Ruby?" my four-year-old granddaughter asked me one day, while gently stroking the head of our salt and pepper Miniature Schnauzer.

We were sitting on the couch in my home. Her question came out of nowhere, a strange interruption to our conversation about what to have for snack. I shouldn't have been surprised. A few hours earlier while we were shopping at the mall, she had asked me about her great-grandma.

"So, what do you think great-grandma and Jesus are doing?" Her question had caught me off guard, as we glided past racks of women's clothing, my attention drifting aimlessly.

Now, her saucer-sized brown eyes held a particular seriousness as she searched my face for clues. Behind all her curiosity seemed to be the perception of a bigger story, a holy hunch.

Sometimes I forget the power of these little mystics in our midst, how they pull down things of heaven in the middle of the ordinary, how their hearts so freely and easily pulse with vibrations of eternity.

"Well," I began slowly, "before you were born, your uncle Nate was really, really sick. We thought a little puppy would help him feel better."

"Sick?" she asked, completely puzzled, blinking. "How sick?"

"Really sick," I said. "Like lying-on-this-couch-all-day kind of sick," I said, patting the weathered leather sectional.

How do you explain brain cancer to a four-year-old?

The truth is, it's still hard for me to grasp the story that happened to us nine years ago. Then, our twenty-one-year-old-son, Nate, was diagnosed with cancer in the form of an inoperable brainstem tumor.

The tumor was located in the most delicate region of the human body—"ground zero," said the neurosurgeon. Inoperable meant there was no cutting it out, no de-bulking the thing with a scalpel or gamma ray. Quite simply, no way back to hope. Medical science did everything they could through aggressive radiation and the strongest chemotherapy to delay its advance.

This is a story about hope.

In a time when cancer claims lives like an insidious leviathan, this story speaks of a different ending. And such endings are so very necessary when our experience tells us differently.

I have lost a father, two mothers, and a dear friend at fifty-two to the ending most familiar to us. I watched each one in their last days with cancer, becoming a shell of who they once were in body, mind, and spirit. It is heartbreaking.

Many of us know firsthand the grief that grips the heart and dries the mouth like an arid wasteland. These are the stories we most regularly tell, that settle deep into the marrow of our bones and sap our lifeblood.

I know. We know.

During the course of our journey, our family heard versions of such stories repeated by a thousand different tongues. "Brain cancer," people would say, shaking their heads only to launch into wretched tales of anguish about another person's experience with the lethal disease.

And with their words—part anecdotal gibberish to fill the awkward moment, part reckless appropriation of another's life—the oxygen of hope would evaporate. We who were in the midst of the struggle would fall into dumb silence.

So, to tell a different story is to proclaim a new possibility, to point toward a frontier where the Author of Life has a chance to surprise and astonish our rational and all-but-withered sensibilities. A shoot can spring forth from a field of stumps. New life can yet be raised up against all medical odds.

This is a story about faith.

The faith in these pages is sometimes tattered, sometimes tough, sometimes tethered to God by a thread. It is a faith that doubts, soars, sits wounded and bruised on an ash heap, begging for answers from a silent, starry universe. It is a faith formed in suffering—difficult to describe and altogether sacred. It is a faith that holds a thousand losses and loses all certainty.

It is a story about *my* faith.

A child with cancer is a radical upset to the natural order of things. It exposes all that is wrong in the world. And it highlights our malignant beliefs about God, which are often the result of a comfortable existence.

Before cancer, mine was a faith with answers, a faith that stayed safe and didn't bleed. But comfort and safety are never promised.

Faith that comes to us and calls itself *Christian* is cruciform—in the shape of a cross—with a God-man who was pierced. In suffering, we share in the wounds of Christ. Here, faith holds only to mystery and the promise that what dies will rise.

This is a story about mercy.

Mercy is such an old-fashioned word. It's not part of our everyday vocabulary, like, say, the word blessed, which has devolved into something closer to "luck." #Blessed—the catchall for everything from a convenient parking spot at Costco to a Rocky Mountain ski vacation.

No. The word *mercy* is still hallowed, full of its original meaning and goodness. It comes to us in ancient liturgy whispered most often by the faithful at prayer.

*Lord have mercy. Christ have mercy.*

According to the ancient stories of our faith, mercy fills the universe; it is at the very center of human existence. It is God's very essence. His breath in us. Hebrew scripture calls it *hesed*, a lovingkindness that infuses every atom and molecule, forms matter and meaning, pulses in each heartbeat, and holds each soul in life.

The Hebrews used another word, too, to get at the marrow of this mercy. The word is *racham*, a womb-like love that moves in and toward us with tenderness, gathering our shivering frames under her great and mighty wingspan, offering protection and refuge, scrubbing us clean, singing over us, gazing at us with eyes that dance with delight.

Maternal mercy. Could it be true? What if divine love is more like mother-love, altogether involved, ever longing for intimacy, always giving generously of herself for the sake of her child. How might that change the way we imagine God?

One day we will understand the mercy that shaped our lives, that came to us in the dark night, wrapped around us, steadied our step in the valley of shadow, and carried us. Someday we will know the fullness of the mercy that met us in our suffering hour. On that day, there will be no degree of separation, only union.

Until then, we look for this holy presence that occupies time and space and makes its home in the human heart. We are watchers together for these "gifts wrapped in darkness,"[1] for mercy in all its misty forms—promised new every morning, saving us again and again.

*Lord have mercy. Christ have mercy.*

This book will trace the shape of mercy that transfused our sorrow with bits and bursts of joy, and changed the shape of our lives. During the precarious months and years of Nate's illness, mercy was sometimes wrapped tiny, a wisp of a thing, poised on the tip of a finger. Other times,

---

1. Chittister and Williams, *Uncommon Gratitude*, viii.

mercy was wrapped wild, coming unexpected in a dream, a vision, an MRI image scrubbed clean. Once, mercy came covered with dirt, through a patch of land and open water.

Most times though, mercy came wrapped in skin, with a name, a person who showed up, bearing kindness.

Make no mistake, mercy does not arrive wrapped in a bow. It's not obvious like that. But if we hold open our hearts, even a crack, mercy can slip in and surprise us.

You may come to these pages with curiosity or desperation, skepticism or plain hunger for hope. Whatever it is, may you find something here that feels like firm footing, a place to stand. And may you find, in your own story, the shape of mercy.

# 1

## Holy Messenger

**ANNUNCIATION**

a holy messenger
painted in thin wisps of glory
orange and black and spotted white
made of pure splendor
shuddering in flight
comes strangely close
pausing to fan delicate its opaque wings on the tip of a finger
bringing all heaven to bleak earth
lingering long enough to proclaim
"eternity is joined to your suffering
the Creator is present
fear not"

—JAN WOLTMANN

A POSTER ON THE fifth-floor step-down unit of the hospital glared down at me: *A brain tumor changes everything*. The haunting faces of a couple, maybe in their early thirties, filled the frame, unsmiling. I began to shiver. My son's face will not be on the next poster, I vowed. I turned away. How did we get *here*? I thought back . . . .

It was the August long weekend, the midsummer divide that signals a turn in the season. We were spending three lazy days with our kids at my husband's family cottage, located an hour north of Winnipeg on a stretch of the planet's most gorgeous beaches.

It was just the six of us—my husband, Norm; our daughter Laura and her husband, Jeff; our daughter Kate, and our son, Nate. No extended family this time.

We did the usual things—beaching, biking, binge-snacking. Our older kids took full advantage of the sunshine and wide-open spaces. But our youngest didn't participate like the others.

Nate had what seemed like a bad stomach virus in the days prior to, and during, our lake weekend. He would wake up nauseated, vomit a few times and feel better for a stretch of hours. He even biked a six-mile route to the local store with us. Norm and I tossed around the idea that it could be a bad case of sunstroke, but it seemed strange that it had hung on this long.

On Monday afternoon, as a precaution, I took Nate to a walk-in clinic. It seemed like the best option on a civic holiday.

Nate checked out fine according to the doctor, even though he vomited when we got to the clinic. No abnormalities in his abdomen, nothing wrong with his hearing or sight. The doctor gave us a requisition for bloodwork and sent us on our way. I felt temporarily relieved.

The week progressed, but Nate showed little sign of improvement. The recurring nausea was worst at night and he would wake to vomit.

In retrospect, I probably should have taken him to the family doctor, or straight to emergency. Or, with the full illumination of hindsight, we immediately should have driven eight hours south to the Mayo Clinic in Minnesota. But Nate's bouts of vomiting cleared up considerably during the day. He went to his summer job every morning that week, and even managed to enroll for his third year in the business program at the University of Winnipeg.

The following weekend, however, Nate's condition worsened considerably. Overnight, his vision changed.

A year or so earlier, an ophthalmologist had diagnosed Nate with a mild case of double vision. Nate's condition was identified as a fourth nerve palsy, the weakening of a particular nerve, thought to be caused by genetic factors or a number of minor occurrences, such as a bump to the head. Nate had suffered a nasty bicycle accident when he was ten, which seemed to be a satisfactory explanation at the time. In any case, the doctor was not alarmed; the condition was not considered serious. The doctor had prescribed prism lenses to unify Nate' vision and allow him to go about life as usual.

Until now.

On this mid-August weekend, Nate's double vision morphed into distortions vertically and horizontally—he was seeing shadow images above, below and off to the side. What's more, his right eyeball had shifted slightly and would not follow normally.

We scheduled an appointment with the optometrist for Monday afternoon. I went to work that morning, our lost innocence looming on the horizon.

I had taken a job the previous year with my church's national office as a writer. After a routine meeting, I rehearsed Nate's symptoms and poured out my fears to a colleague. Within earshot was an older gentleman whom I had come to love by the name of Bert. He possessed a deep treasure of faith that bubbled up in wisdom and kindness, with a generous dose of Scottish merriment.

But on this day, Bert's tone was even and completely serious. "God is able," he said, his arms folded in front of him and eyes holding mine in an unflinching gaze.

Bert's words stilled me and would return often over the course of the coming months. I would later learn that Bert possessed a secret knowing—he had walked closely with a young pastor who recently died of a brain tumor.

After checking and re-checking Nate's eyes, the optometrist sounded the alarm, suggesting a full battery of medical tests. I could feel the internal panic rising when I called Norm and then again when I spoke with our good friend, Warren, an orthopedic surgeon. Although quite confident it was not necessarily serious, Warren scheduled Nate for an MRI within forty-eight hours.

OUR WORLD WAS UNRAVELLING quickly.

On Tuesday afternoon, daughter Kate experienced a serious trauma of another kind. Our free-spirited twenty-three-year-old had been spending the balance of her free time that summer perfecting her skills as a dirt biker, in part to impress a young man. On this day, she was participating in a dirt bike competition. But the race ended abruptly after the first corner, when Kate's bike slid out from underneath her body. She sustained a severe injury, tearing all the ligaments in her right knee.

MRIs for both children occurred back-to-back in the next twenty-four hours.

On the outside, I was trying desperately to stay calm, fragments of prayers and pleadings moving through my consciousness like wisps of vapor. But there was a growing sense that we were entering a full-blown crisis, the extent of which would prove to be a *ten* on the Richter scale, if such crises could be measured by earthquake standards. God help us.

Nate's MRI results arrived on Friday. Norm received a call from Warren just after lunch.

"I'm on my way to your house," he said. "Is Jan with you?"

"No, she's running errands," Norm replied.

"Tell her to come home," said Warren. "The three of you need to hear this news in person. I'm afraid it's not good."

Norm and I sat on either side of our son, a physical shield to somehow help him absorb this moment that would forever change us.

"You've got a brain tumor, Nathan," Warren said, his eyes filled with compassion as he sat on the footstool facing us. "It's the size of a small marble and it's located in your brainstem, the most delicate and problematic of places. There's no surgery that can be done to remove it. At this point it looks non-aggressive, but nothing can be ruled out yet."

The three of us sat transfixed, disbelieving, afraid to move.

"But there's a more immediate concern" he said urgently, his voice quivering, his hands folded together, his body leaning toward us.

"Your brain is filling up with fluid because of the mass. The condition is called hydrocephalus," Warren said. This explained the nausea and vomiting, a gastro-neurological response to the abnormal volume of fluid passing through the ventricles, which in turn put pressure on the optic nerve, distorting Nate's vision.

"Surgery needs to happen soon," he said. "A neurosurgeon will consult with you first thing Monday morning."

With that, our friend hugged each of us and went on his way.

"Crisis happens when the ordinary turns deadly on us, veers off the road, lands us upside down on the path we had long taken for granted and cuts us off from the predictable, the regular, the expected, the ordinary part of life,"[1] writes Benedictine nun and author Joan Chittister.

Our lives were careening off the edge of ordinary in that moment.

And what of mercy? Mercy is the very life force of God within and around us that sustains the next breath; enables us to huddle close, hug long,

---

1. Chittister and Williams, *Uncommon Gratitude*, 135.

get up and do the next necessary thing. Just that one thing. And it's the palpable sense we're not alone in the task.

When suffering threatens to suffocate hope, a fierce mercy wraps its arms around us and gently pulls us forward. It is a mystery that knows no words but arrives daily. It is anything but ordinary.


AND SO WE DO the next necessary thing and gather our children. Laura, Jeff, and Kate complete the circle as we put words to the results.

Brain tumor. The term feels wretched and foreign even as we repeat it throughout the conversation. My mouth is dry and tears come easily. It is late afternoon now, and the dinner hour has come and gone. We order Chinese food in an attempt to regain some energy. Food is fuel; there is nothing that awakens the taste buds, nothing that awakens much of anything in this numbness.

We disperse to different corners of our home to make phone calls to family and close friends. Closed doors, hushed tones, private conversations.

We don't want to disturb Nate during these exchanges. I call my parents in Saskatchewan and my two older brothers in Winnipeg. I struggle to believe anything that comes out of my mouth. This cannot be our story.

Several friends come to be with us that evening. Nate is especially passionate and speaks at length about the peace he feels; how close Jesus is. He is not fond of reading, but in recent weeks he's read two books about faith in crisis. Both have stirred his soul and ignited his imagination, as if preparing him for this moment.

We gather around him. In a custom familiar and comforting to us, we put our hands on him and pray. It is the prayer of our longtime friend, Willy, that captures my attention. He prays for the miraculous, that the tumor would vanish and Nate's sight would be restored. "Yes, and amen," I whisper in my heart of hearts. "God is able," I hear Bert echo.

Norm and I are utterly exhausted, yet sleep eludes us.

We stay close to one another as the weekend unfolds. Saturday, Nate shares the news with his buddies and we go about the day as best we can. On Sunday, our hearts feel heavier as the reality of our circumstances penetrates deeper into our consciousness.

Norm and I talk and cry as we put together our list of questions for the neurosurgeon the next morning. Fear is setting in, taking hold of our imaginations during the waking hours and catapulting us into catastrophe.

Norm's extended family offers support that evening—another small mercy that reminds us we are not alone in this task—aunts, uncles, and cousins circle around our son to anoint Nate's head with oil and pray. This practice of praying for the sick, common within our Christian community, is a tender reminder of God's presence with us. Somehow the family's fierce faith quells our fears and we go to our beds encouraged and hopeful.

It is the first time we see it for ourselves. A cloudy little patch of mass on the image of an otherwise healthy brain. The neurosurgeon points it out, and I am sickened by the sight of it. That is my son's brain on the computer screen and my mamma-heart desperately tries to remain rational in this surreal moment. It takes every ounce of internal fortitude to stay calm in order to ask good questions.

I frantically write down the words I hear: slow-growing, glioma, enmeshed with healthy brain tissue, measuring a little over two centimeters, extremely swollen ventricles. A gamma knife would be of no help; a biopsy is out of the question. Radiation may be an option, but given the tumor's location in the most vulnerable area of the brain, there's no guarantee Nate's eyesight would be restored.

"There are no quick fixes," says the surgeon. And with that, he dismisses us into our night.

"To some extent, we can assume that various dimensions of the night are always going on in our lives," explains psychiatrist Gerald May in his book *The Dark Night of the Soul*. "God is always working obscurely within us. And even more mysteriously, some part of us is saying yes to God's invitation to go where we do not want to go."[2]

And so it seems for Nate.

A heaviness settles over us. As we drive, Nate begins to weep. He doesn't want to die but feels prepared for heaven. These words scorch my already deep-down ache—I can't bear to hear his pain and am overcome with sorrow as I hear him struggle to put words to his faith, his trust, his surrender.

I cannot muster many words. Hope is all but suffocated in the cab of our truck, and groaning is all that befits prayer. With tears, we convey the latest news to our other kids.

Later that same afternoon, I get a call from the neurosurgeon. A group of specialists have met to discuss Nate's case and are excited about a new development that could provide more information about the nature of the tumor. As part of the surgery to create a conduit for the excess brain fluid, they propose sending a probe down one of the ventricles, now swollen to four times its normal size, in order to collect a "nibble" of the tumor. The neurosurgeon assures me this procedure—a ventricular tumor biopsy—could

2. May, *The Dark Night of the Soul*, 95.

provide an extremely rare and relatively safe opportunity for an accurate diagnosis. A sliver of good news.

Nate and Norm are floating around the backyard pool in the August sunshine. When Nate hears the news about the procedure, he shakes with both fear and excitement. He trembles because he is all too aware of the risks attached to any kind of surgery that involves the brain: damage to the memory banks, injury to the nerve tissue that controls fine and gross motor movement, an altered personality. All are possibilities if the surgery does not go as expected.

Seventy-two hours have passed since we received the MRI results. Enough time for our hearts to be broken open. Enough time to reckon with the fact that the world we have lived in until now is quickly coming apart.

Wasn't it just last week that I waited on the university campus for Nate to register for his fall courses? Yes, and it was still early August. Maybe, just maybe, if everything went well with the surgery, and there were no complications during recovery, Nate could take one or two of those courses. Yes, I thought, that may yet be possible.

"Struggle begins with shock. With loss. With radical interruption of what just moments before had been certain and sure and drowsily eternal,"[3] says Joan Chittister.

Into this moment, hope appears, a kind of annunciation. It lands at the edge of the pool in the form of a monarch—resplendent in color, with elegant wings aflutter.

With a faint whistle, my husband beckons the butterfly saying, "Come here and join our conversation." To their astonishment, the monarch takes flight and settles on Norm's finger. Minutes pass and the creature just sits there, fixing its gaze on our son. All the while, its large wings gracefully rise and fall to the rhythm of its Choreographer.

Time seems at a standstill now, wonder flooding the fearful places. That butterfly gaze brings with it a divine gaze that holds our deepest trembling. God sees. God knows. Into our night, enough light shines through those translucent wings to reveal hope and the promise of Presence. Suddenly, the August air smells fresh and colors shimmer. The invisible has infused the visible, and we are fully awake. Mercy feels like this.

Mercy feels and looks like "symbols that arrive at just the right time." Symbols become for us the doorway to all we need to know, "allowing us to move beyond complexity and illusion,"[4] explains Richard Rohr, notable writer in the field of Christian contemplative spirituality.

3. Chittister, *Scarred By Struggle*, 21.
4. Rohr, *Immortal Diamond*, 70.

From this day onward, the monarch, our holy messenger of hope, will be our ever-opening symbol. A doorway to knowing that God is here, fully attentive and altogether involved.

In just a few weeks, our delicate mid-August monarch will make an unspeakable journey southward, following a flight path stretching over thousands of miles. In the months and years to come, we, too, will make an unspeakable journey.

But never will we travel alone.

# 2

# Gotcha

Communion with God in the silence of the heart is a God-given capacity, like the rhododendron's capacity to flower, the fledgling's for flight, and the child's for self-forgetful abandon and joy.

—Martin Laird[1]

To this day there are two scars on his head—one visible, the length of a postage stamp above his right eye, and the other out of sight, on top of his scalp. They are reminders of a deep physical struggle that began with brain surgery on August 17, 2011.

Then, he was a tall, tanned twenty-one-year-old admitted to the hospital wearing his favorite white T-shirt and blue jeans. I can still hear the nurses on the step-down unit cooing over him, saying he looked far too healthy to be admitted as a patient.

And they were right, except for the presence of a two-centimeter tumor on his upper brainstem, a little tangle of normal brain tissue enmeshed with a pathological collection of cells.

During our surgical debrief the previous day, we had met with the neurosurgeon, the second specialist to see us in the span of seventy-two hours. He had expressed surprise that a tumor this size had not wreaked more havoc for Nate.

1. Laird, *Into the Silent Land*, 1.

An expansive grace it would seem, along with the news that this kind of tumor, likely childhood in origin, could remain stable for years, even decades. We would learn that primary brain tumors, those that start in the brain rather than elsewhere in the body, could either be benign or malignant. The latter was cancerous, usually fast-growing and life-threatening.

Benign tumors, on the other hand, were slow-growing. And although they could cause trouble (especially in the delicate regions of the brainstem), they could also stay static for long stretches of time. Every part of our fragile hope hung on to that speculation, although the doctor couldn't be sure. The biopsy would provide important clues.

The neurosurgeon's team would perform an endoscopic third ventriculostomy. It would involve two incisions into the skull to insert a pencil-sized scope through the most delicate circuitry in the human brain. In addition to collecting a small sample of the tumor via the stretched ventricles, the doctors would create a dime-sized hole at the bottom of the third ventricle to allow for drainage. The excess fluid that was damaging Nate's vision was now reaching dangerous levels and needed somewhere to go. If left untreated, Nate would die within days.

I pictured him in the field where he worked, alone with his grass trimmer, his brain bulging with water, his body lying limp on the ground. A shudder rippled down my spine.

But what shocked us into silence was the dreadful list of surgical risks: chance of death, damage to the memory structures, paralysis, permanent vegetative state, bleeding from a major artery. The neurosurgeon described the procedure as "the least worst way of getting at the tumor tissue" so pathology could determine next steps.

We quickly discovered that within these medical walls, words were measured—dealt with the same precision and clarity as a scalpel. We would need to look elsewhere for words of comfort.

As the surgical debrief unfolded, we all seemed to wilt under the sheer volume of information. Nate had made it clear to us that he did not want to hear about the risks involved.

But, as a young adult, it was Nate's responsibility to be informed about every facet of his case. This would prove to be an enormous weight for a body and mind that had just barely come of age.

We waited twenty-four hours in the step-down unit before Nate was admitted to surgery. It was enough time for the wild beasts of fear and terror to regurgitate the surgeon's vile list of risks over and over again. Enough time for our imaginations to conjure up images that left our bodies clenched and sweaty. Enough time to see the poster in the hospital hallway with its foreboding message: *A brain tumor changes everything.*

We would soon understand that brain surgery is categorically different from all other surgical procedures done to protect the body. Repairing a limb or scoping an internal organ are serious, to be sure, but prodding inside the brain introduces a level of risk all its own.

For within the brain lives a person's very identity—the personality that determines his or her way of being in the world, the ability to decode language and communicate, the capacity to empathize with oneself or another, the desire to respond with a smile. These are the basic functions of life that give shape and meaning to a shared humanity.

An individual's very soul is under threat of collapse should a scope or scalpel move even a millimeter off course. Neurosurgery, I have come to believe, is nothing less than a holy endeavor.

Nate lay fitfully in his hospital bed hooked up to an intravenous pole, ready at a moment's notice for surgery. At times, the fear would rise to unbearable levels. Norm held his hand with a steadfast grip through the watches of the night and never left his side.

I lay beside him throughout the day and did my best to ease his mental anguish by rubbing his back and neck, offering words of comfort and short prayers.

But something else gave him comfort. And this was mercy: the word *Gotcha.* It came from a deep reservoir within Nate's being. It repeated itself with resounding clarity in his consciousness.

*Gotcha* was its simple message. Each time the surgical risks scrolled like a horror movie on the screen of his mind, the still, small voice would say *Gotcha.* Arriving into this moment of wrestling and growing in intensity with each passing hour, the word provided relief.

Wielding this word like a medieval sword, Nate met each and every "what if" and cut off its power to disturb. The phrase provided so much comfort and peace that Nate was finally able to sleep for a few hours during the night and for small stretches in the hours preceding surgery.

Our son was wheeled to the operating room at four o'clock that afternoon. Nate's word became a comfort for us, too, as we waited through the long hours of surgery. It was apparent that God was the author of this word that carried Nate through his dark night. God came closer than his breathing, closer than his thinking, closer even than his choosing. *Gotcha.*

God came close enough to wield power in the form of two simple syllables that stilled the turbulence within the mind of a terrified twenty-one-year-old. I would learn in the coming years that the use of such a word or phrase was a form of Christian prayer that reached back through the centuries.

MORE THAN 600 YEARS ago, an anonymous English monk wrote a book called *The Cloud of Unknowing.* The book is full of practical wisdom for those who desire to experience the deep reaches of God's love. It is considered a spiritual classic in Christian literature and has inspired legends of the faith such as St. John of the Cross, Pierre Teilhard de Chardin, and more recently Thomas Keating. The treasures in its pages are available to those who wish to open themselves more deeply to God through quiet and still prayer— contemplative in nature.

But as *The Cloud's* author well knows, stilling the chattering mind challenges the most devout in any century. So, he gently and plainly offers instruction to help his readers find a way to quietly listen for God. Tucked away in the center of the book, he writes:

> Take just a little word, of one syllable rather than of two; for the shorter it is the better it is in agreement with this exercise of the spirit. Such a one is the word "God" or the word "love." Choose which one you prefer, or any other according to your liking— the word of one syllable that you like best. Fasten this word to your heart, so that whatever happens it will never go away. This word is to be your shield and your spear, whether you are riding in peace or in war. This word you are to beat upon this cloud and this darkness above you. With this word you are to strike down every kind of thought under the cloud of forgetting; so that if any thought should press upon you and ask you what you would have, answer it with no other word but with this one . . . If you will hold fast to this purpose, you may be sure that the thought will not stay for very long.[2]

Today's contemplative Christian writers call this a *sacred word* or a *prayer word.*

Now, five years later, as I read *The Cloud's* description of a prayer word, I am astonished by how closely the author seems to describe Nate's experience. That night in his hospital room, our son had no context for this condensed form of prayer, and the process of consciously choosing a prayer word was beyond his capacity.

So it seems that God, in his mercy, created it for Nate. Somewhere from within, hovering over the tempest of Nate's toxic and terrifying thoughts, God's Spirit spoke the word into being and "fastened it to his heart." And fastened it tightly.

I think the author of *The Cloud* would smile, maybe even chuckle at a sacred word like *Gotcha.* It is certainly unconventional, and clearly not

---

2. Walsh, *The Cloud of Unknowing*, 134.

found in Christian scripture. Yet the word possesses the kind of holy presence and power that could capture the imagination of a young man who had spent more time contemplating dirt bike trails than holy directives.

As a mother, I am familiar with fierce love. I will step in harm's way if it so much as looks sideways at my child. Yet, even now, I wonder if that which I consider fierce love pales in comparison to divine love—love that is knit into our primal being long before birth.

"It was you who formed my inward parts; you knit me together in my mother's womb," whispers the biblical writer. "My frame was not hidden from you, when I was being made in secret, intricately woven in the depths of the earth" (Psalm 139:13–15, RSV).

Together with the wide-eyed author of Psalm 139, I am filled with wonder at these most intimate and maternal movements within the heart of God that causes each cell of our naked being to take shape and be known.

"Long before any human being saw us, we are seen by God's loving eyes," says Henri Nouwen in his beautiful book *Life of the Beloved*. "Long before anyone heard us cry or laugh, we are heard by our God who is all ears for us. Long before any person spoke to us in this world, we are spoken to by the voice of eternal love. Our preciousness, uniqueness, and individuality are not given to us by those who meet us in clock-time—our brief chronological existence—but by the One who has chosen us with an everlasting love, a love that existed from all eternity."[3]

And after we're born, there remains an unseen and utterly divine umbilical cord attached to our deepest center, fierce in its desire to nourish and sustain us through our earthly pilgrimage.

And what is that deepest center if not our heart? It is not the human organ that pumps blood to our body, or the sentimental construct found in a drugstore card. Ancient Hebrew writers, such as the author of Psalm 139, understand the heart differently. For them, it represents a person's core—the place that is deeper than our thinking or feeling, where we discover ourselves found and completely loved by God.

It's not surprising, then, that this intimate link becomes very real in our hour of suffering. When we suffer on a sickbed of terminal proportions, we are brought to a vulnerable stillness. It is not a stillness chosen amidst the clamor of the everyday. Not a stillness practiced as a form of prayer by the devout. Rather, it is a stillness, stripped of ego and self-sufficiency, which opens the heart to reach for its first and deepest connection.

---

3. Nouwen, *Life of the Beloved*, 58.

The evening that Nate was admitted to the hospital, our pastor read Psalm 139. In the formidable stillness that followed, mercy delivered the assurance of presence to Nate's deepest center and fastened a word to his heart. In his core, Nate discovered himself already found by God. In his core, he received the gift of a sacred word to combat all that would rise up to oppose the life-force of God within.

This is fierce love. Perhaps this is what the ancients had in mind when they spoke of God's mercy as *racham*, the womb-like love of the Almighty that follows us all the days of our lives—from birth, even unto death.[4]

"Textbook case," says the neurosurgeon after three torturous hours, and ushers us to the post-surgical unit.

Nate is conscious, although still somewhat groggy from the anesthesia. He recognizes us and speaks coherently, even joking about the draft he feels in his lower regions. A young nurse is present, and laughs at his antics.

Gratitude overwhelms me as I witness his normalcy. He is most certainly our Nate on every level. "Thanks be to God," I whisper.

The next day, I decorate Nate's room with get well cards and a few fresh cut flowers.

"It's the end of the beginning," says the neurosurgeon when he visits Nate's room on his rounds. I raise a quizzical eyebrow but he doesn't explain. What an odd thing to say. What does that even mean? The poster makes a brief reappearance in my mind's eye before I swat away the thought. *Stop analyzing.* I smile at the boy sleeping in the bed.

Tough days of recovery follow. Intense head pain and constant vomiting are results of the trauma to his brain. I replay the recent events, and remember the surgeon's explanation that such tumors originate in childhood.

As I helplessly watch Nate suffer in that hospital room, I see images of him as a toddler chasing after his sisters; then as a young boy of ten, his blond hair, bright eyes, and lithe body chasing a soccer ball in the front yard with his dad.

Accompanying these images is the retrospective knowledge that something unseen was growing in his brain that I could not prevent.

Although a futile exercise, I want to know when the tumor began to exist alongside our innocence.

And what about Nate's future? University graduation? A career in business? Marriage? A family? Would these dreams find flight?

---

4. Trible, *God and the Rhetoric of Sexuality*, 33.

Into my cascade of questions comes a gentle reminder of a greater love that precedes my own. A love that was present and altogether involved in knitting each of Nate's cells and ligaments together inside my body. God knew and loved him long before my time with him began. This was his holy origin. The hands that molded and shaped my son were now holding us in our heartache, helping us cope in the midst of a tectonic life-change. *Gotcha!*

LAURA MANAGES TO BRING Kate, recovering from her knee surgery, into the hospital by wheelchair. The two sisters are a comical sight as they make their way down the corridor to Nate's room. Kate offers a winsome smile to all who greet her along the way, while Laura steers them responsibly through the hallway traffic.

The girls bounce into the room full of stories about the perils of wheelchair travel on uneven sidewalks and in crowded elevators. Their hilarity dispels the density of our wordless vigil and provides a necessary tonic.

My heart is completely warmed by their sisterly solidarity and the enormous effort they have made to be at their brother's side. I recognize the mighty women that live inside each of these daughters of mine. I revel in the light and love they bring into the room.

As I leave the hospital later that evening, Nate, who has been groggy and nauseous all day, speaks a declaration. "I will not die but live and proclaim the goodness of the Lord," he says, repeating the words of Psalm 118. His eyes are closed; his determination is unwavering. My heart comes undone.

That night, I lie face down on the floor, crying out my grief and tension to the Christ of my life. The echo of Nate's declaration arrives into the heartbreak: "I will not die but live and proclaim the goodness of the Lord."

I want so desperately to believe this for now and for the future, but doubt confronts my faith. There is still an inoperable tumor in Nate's brainstem—one that is supposedly benign and slow-growing. We won't know for sure until that biopsy report arrives.

I recall the scene with Martha and Jesus after the death of Lazarus, recorded in the Gospel of John. In the midst of this most intimate and theological exchange, I hear Jesus console and challenge Martha with the statement that *he* embodies resurrection life. I hear Martha declare her faith in the future resurrection and her brother's place in it.

But I also hear the ache in Martha's voice that grieves Lazarus' absence for the remainder of her earthly days. This is lament.

In that moment, I am Martha. I hear a tender voice telling me that life will always follow death. And I am consoled that Nate, even if he should die, is destined for more life than we know. But like Martha, I still want him here.

Jesus knows these groans and hears my request to extend my son's life. I dare to remember what comes next: the raising of Lazarus to life, and not just in the hereafter.

The story allows a crack of light into the darkness and disorientation of my spirit. And I dare to wonder whether such a wondrous resurrection could happen for us.

NATE'S HOMECOMING IS JOYOUS but altogether stressful. He experiences head pain and nausea, and is overwhelmed by everyday noises. We work hard to fight exhaustion and keep the household quiet. It is important to stay on top of his medications. There are two bald patches where the doctors shaved his head and stitched his skin. The eye that sees multiple images is covered with medical gauze and tape so it won't cause further disorientation.

Nate is not the same young man who entered the hospital five days ago. At night, he sleeps on a mattress on our bedroom floor so Norm can wake him and administer pain medication. During the day, Nate sleeps downstairs on the couch.

The last time we brought our son home from the hospital, he was an infant: joy, gratitude, hope, and future were all wrapped up in that little bundle of boy. Fear, heartache, pain, and uncertainty are the stuff of this experience. The two life moments stand in stark contrast.

IN THE WEEKS THAT follow, Nate's strength slowly returns. We take evening drives to the countryside, the three of us. That's when Nate's thoughts tumble out.

He tells us how much more he appreciates life; he marvels at the sunset and the deer that darts across the road. At least he can see these things, even if he sees double of them. Gratitude bubbles out of Nate. He talks about feeling fully alive. He knows his faith is being tested so severely, yet still he hears God speak lovingly over him.

One night, during a dramatic prairie thunderstorm, Nate kneels at our bedroom window at 3:00 a.m. to watch it unfold. Creation has always been Nate's pathway to God. A question comes to Nate with clarity: "Do you trust me?" As Nate ponders his response, the sky breaks open with lightning— sheet lightning and fork lightning on spectacular display. Doubt is silenced by the sheer wonder and power of the cosmos. *Gotcha*, it seems to say, with all the force of the universe in agreement.

The next morning, Nate is alive with possibility and fresh revelation.

His attitude mystifies me. His maturity is staggering. Nate becomes my teacher. My son becomes mercy to me.

I believe Jesus comes particularly near the brokenhearted. Our family is brokenhearted, our emotions jagged. Somehow, in that brokenness, surrounded by the shards of a once-familiar life, courage arrives as a companion. Courage to rise to another day and even eat a few bites from whatever is on the counter or in the fridge.

What's more, we find courage to recognize and bind every moment of ordinary goodness to memory like a delicate graft of a twig to a tree. This capacity to be awake to the present moment, fully awake to the "now," carves out a deeper place inside.

"The essence of struggle," writes Joan Chittister, "is neither endurance or denial. The essence of struggle is the decision to become new rather than simply become older. It's the opportunity to grow either smaller or larger in the process."[5]

Nate is growing larger, and at a pace we can hardly keep up with. Nate is mercy!

5. Chittister, *Scarred by Struggle*, 23.

# 3

# Conversion

Events happen under their own steam as random as rain, which means that God is present in them not as their cause but as the one who even in the hardest and most hair-raising of them offers us the possibility of that new life and healing which I believe is what salvation is.

—FREDERICK BUECHNER[1]

THE OFFICIAL-LOOKING LETTER THAT arrived on September 2 was addressed to Nate, but the return address on the envelope was mystifying. The fancy script caused a wave of fear to pass through me. Judging from the terse message inside, the letter appeared to be computer generated, from a doctor I had never even heard of.

Nate's full name appeared at the top of the letter, beside the bold script that read *Patient*. My eyes skimmed the content and fixed on the acronym "CCMB" and the name "Dr. Gerald Schneider."

CCMB—CancerCare Manitoba. CancerCare? "This must be a mistake," I protested loudly in an effort to calm my wild thoughts. *Not a follow-up at the neurology clinic at the hospital? It can't be! It was supposed to be benign.*

---

1. Buechner, *Telling Secrets*, 31.

CancerCare. That's where they had sent us to receive the results of Nate's biopsy. CancerCare. The name itself announced doom. Patients went there when the diagnosis was dark and the news grim.

CancerCare was an imposing structure attached to the hospital, with a three-story wall of windows on the east side. The beauty of its architecture could not eclipse the pain and sadness that lived inside.

We walked down the main hallway that spanned the length of the building, passing clinics along the way. Tables with wigs, brochures and support material flanked the breast cancer clinic. The brain tumor clinic was near the end. It had a spacious waiting area with large cushioned chairs.

Behind the wall of the reception desk was an oversized room that served as the hub for doctors, nurses, and support workers. The small clinic rooms formed a u-shape around its perimeter.

After checking in, the three of us were seated in a corner room. It was stark, equipped with a small desk, examination bed, and several chairs. We huddled together, holding hands and holding our breath while the minutes stretched out like miles.

Finally, the door opened. In walked Dr. Schneider, the radiation oncologist who specialized in plans and treatments.

Short in stature, his white coat hanging frumpishly off his small body, baggy sleeves rolled up past the elbows, Schneider cut a quirky figure. Probably in his mid-fifties, he was self-possessed, with bushy eyebrows, fleshy jowls, and an eye that didn't seem to focus properly. *Dear God Almighty*, I inwardly gasped. A modern-day Mr. Magoo!

"Hello," he said in a cheery tone.

And that was the end of the small talk.

We must have been a sight, the three of us huddled together in the clinic chairs holding hands, our bodies stiff and bracing for bad news, our eyes full of dread. No doubt he recognized the fear. With lightening quickness, he sat down and opened Nate's file.

"I'm not sure why you were sent here," he said in a puzzled tone. "This meeting seems premature."

Dr. Schneider opened the manila folder and mumbled through the report in front of him, reacquainting himself with its content.

"Atypical nuclei are abnormal, but not diagnostic of any kind of a cancer," he announced, reading the conclusion of the report word-for-word.

"No mitosis," he said. "That's where cells are dividing. And there's none."

*No Cancer then? Wait, what?* Had I heard right? "Not diagnostic of any kind of cancer," I repeated out loud in an effort to believe this wildly good news. I looked over at Norm and Nate in that moment, finding confirmation in their expressions.

We *were* in the wrong place!

With this declaration dangling in the air, there suddenly was more oxygen in that little examination room. We let out a collective sigh, signaling it was okay to inhale.

In the minutes that followed, we went back and forth about the terms *malignant* and *benign*, terms that Norm and I had discussed under the cover of darkness when the events of the day were behind us and we would confess the fears that lived at the edge of our existence. We would whisper the word *malignant* in hushed tones, as if it were the most dreadful word in the English vocabulary.

Schneider reiterated the evidence from the report, saying the biopsy tested negative for cells that were dividing, and assuaging our deepest fears that the tumor was malignant.

"But the test is inconclusive," he was quick to add. "Given such a small sample, pathology is not 100 percent positive about what they're dealing with as a whole."

The biopsy had consisted of four pieces of tissue ranging in size from less than 0.1 centimeters up to 0.1 centimeters. The doctors had sent the tissue to British Columbia, to one of the best pathology laboratories in the country. The specimens were reportedly small and not necessarily representative of the tumor tissue as a whole. And while there was evidence of hypercellularity—an abnormal number of cells for the area—there was nothing to indicate they were growing wildly.

"Although I can't be sure," Schneider said, "the findings seem to point to the likely existence of a low-grade astrocytoma, a common primary brain tumor, which develops from star-shaped cells called astocytes.

"This kind could take years to do anything," he declared with a measure of assurance that began to dissolve the mountain of fear we had collected since receiving the letter and news of the appointment.

Before we left, Dr. Schneider gave us his number and invited us to check back with him should we have any questions.

It would be almost three weeks later, at the end of September, before we would have, what should have been, our official post-op appointment with the neurologist.

The time between involved more waiting. Waiting, it seemed, was our primary task in this season.

Our visit to CancerCare, as traumatizing as it was, provided some initial answers. The pathology results left us cautiously encouraged.

But there were still so many lingering questions. Was radiation an option to destroy the tumor tissue? Was chemotherapy a consideration?

A few days later, I picked up the phone and called the number Dr. Schneider had suggested. His nurse answered, and we chatted briefly. She assured me that Dr. Schneider would call back that afternoon.

And he did call, within the hour, which I thought was remarkable given his schedule. He took the time to answer my pressing questions, advising against radiation and chemotherapy because of the nature of Nate's tumor.

Once again, he delivered encouragement—this time, in the form of a story. A young boy had been diagnosed with a tumor similar to Nate's when he was ten. He had received no medical intervention, just follow-up MRIs at regular intervals. The boy was now graduating from high school and pursuing life. We referred to this story many times in the weeks that followed, allowing it to be a pillar of cloud leading us forward through this vast and unknown terrain.

Dr. Schneider's ability to focus on the positive—to keep hope alive—distinguished him from his colleagues and endeared him to our hearts. We didn't know it yet, but this odd little man would embody the measure of mercy we needed for every medical step on this journey.

In the meantime, he would follow up with our neurosurgeon, Dr. Wakefield, and we would await the next step, which was another MRI in two months' time to take further measurements.


ADJUSTMENT TO A NEW normal takes time.

Nate's appearance unsettles him. When friends from high school drop off cookies, he doesn't make eye contact with the two girls. He is self-conscious, realizing he looks like a version of Frankenstein. His hair is shaved, and the ruddy, two-inch black line of stitches on the top of his head has been removed. The incision on his forehead is turning pinkish. The neurosurgeon mentioned that in time, it would become a shiny slit. Not now, though.

Nate has been journaling, too. It had not been his habit, yet this method of self-expression is becoming Nate's way of processing recent events, a way of writing out his grief and prayers—the two co-mingling to form a sacred lament.

On a mid-September day, he reads me an entry.

*I keep hearing a still small voice asking, "Nate, do you trust me?" I don't have an immediate answer, but I keep thinking about the question. The other night, during the thunderstorm, I couldn't sleep so I went to the window and watched it come in. I heard the question again, "Nate, do you trust me?" Suddenly the sky lit up with fork lightning going every which way. I was stunned by this display of power. I told God that I trusted him. I told God that even though I don't know what's ahead, he does and that's good enough.*

As he recalls these moments, he is filled once more with courage to move forward into the uncertainty of the present. Yes, he is grateful for the pathology results and registers caution about getting "too" excited. But here, too, he's grateful. God has answered our prayers for hope and good news in this early diagnosis.

On one of our first outings post-surgery, we go for a short walk among the trees at a spacious park close to our home. It' s soothing to walk the barked path through the woods, quiet and still, away from the indoor monotony.

Nate doesn't miss the opportunity to speak again of living in another dimension in the here-and-now, thankful for eyes to see and ears to hear on this side of surgery. He speaks of how he will never partake in everyday, ordinary activities without acknowledging the marrow of life in each moment.

"Who is this young man?" I wondered to myself.

Yes, faith had been part of his life from the time he was young, but it seemed to operate more in the background rather than at the center. Nate had come to church with us most Sundays through his teen and young adult years, but was not an enthusiastic participant. Most times, it was the promise of a post-church brunch that got him out of bed those mornings.

Nate had always been a great kid by parental standards, exhibiting reasonable, measured decisions when it came to life choices. He was thoughtful and could be reflective from time to time. But conversations of a spiritual nature were certainly not part of our daily exchange.

As parents, Norm and I recognized that our children needed to claim faith as their own. So Nate's apparent ambivalence toward church as a young adult was not unsettling. As long as we stayed in strong relationship with our children, we felt these things would sort themselves out over time. Besides, it was our conviction that God was always at work in hidden and quiet ways.

So, on that afternoon, when my son's vocabulary indicated a seismic internal shift such that he noticed and interpreted the spiritual import of his circumstances, I was dumbfounded.

The shape of his faith was changing.

In the deepest place where the soul ripens, where Nate's should have been springtime green with youth, it was suddenly deep shades of autumn, plump with maturity, aged by suffering and a searing awareness of his own mortality. Gone was the innocence, and in its place something precious was emerging.

"There is then a gift hidden in the travails of forced change," says the sage of struggle, Joan Chittister. "It is the gift of beginning again: conversion."[2] With all its meanings throughout the centuries, conversion is, at its core, a radical and reorienting connection with God, oftentimes revisited again and again during the course of a life. Behold, the old has gone; the new has come, as St. Paul so famously said.

I was a witness to this "forced change"—this transformation of Nate's soul. It was like watching a nature documentary where a time-lapse video reveals in seconds that which takes hours, days or months to record: the flowering of a plant, the birth of an animal, the formation of a storm. What should have been the accumulated wisdom of decades actualized in a matter of weeks.

I allowed my mind to float further back in time.

As an infant, Nate was easily satisfied by food and sleep and short bursts of attention, blissfully content with life. His middle name, Manfred, was given in honor of his Opa, and together with his last name, proudly announced his German heritage. He was the only male in Canada to carry the family name forward.

When he was just two months old, I took the three children on a nine-hour road trip with my parents to my hometown in the center of Saskatchewan. Nate was an exceptional traveler, adapting quickly to circumstances, smiling often and rarely fussy. He traveled through elementary school in a similar fashion.

Nate possessed a tender spirit and on most occasions functioned as the peacemaker between his sisters. When it came to disciplining him in those early years, a disapproving glance from Norm or I would suffice.

At age five, Nate's heart opened to God. He had been listening to a children's story on cassette tape with his sister Laura in our living room. The story detailed the conversion of one of the characters.

"Do you want to ask Jesus to be your forever friend?" Laura asked. And the two of them knelt at the coffee table and folded their hands.

"From all eternity, long before you were born or became a part of history," writes Henri Nouwen, "you existed in God's heart. Long before your parents admired you, or your friends acknowledged your gifts or your

2. Chittister, *Scarred by Struggle*, 23.

teachers, colleagues, and employers encouraged you, you were already 'chosen.'"[3]

Children instinctively know this. They perceive their chosenness, their belonging to God and his angels—that they are somehow inside the heart of a larger Presence. They walk around the world full of astonishment, fresh-faced, souls wide open, captivated by everything small and beautiful along the way. Life has not yet rubbed off the wonder for little ones, they hold within their small selves treasures of the eternal.

Maybe that's why Jesus said, "Truly I tell you, unless you change and become like children, you will never enter the kingdom of heaven."

"This is not an exhortation to become childish, or to nurture one's inner child," writes contemplative author Kathleen Norris about these words of Jesus. "Instead, it reminds us that the grace of childhood lies in being receptive. And to receive as a little child is to receive fully, with an open mind and with gratitude for seemingly limitless nourishment that has come your way."[4]

Nate's athletic prowess was evident early in his development. Nate could dribble a soccer ball up and down the field with both feet when he was five, finding the net with consistent precision, thanks to his dad's coaching. After all, soccer is a beloved game for Germans, and Norm had been an exceptional player until his early twenties.

When Nate entered high school, he turned his attention to volleyball. Again, he excelled, becoming the captain of the team at fifteen. He earned an MVP at a national volleyball event that year and showed extraordinary promise in the sport.

But his dream to play university ball, like his dad, was cut short a year later. During one particularly grueling practice, he injured his back. An MRI showed a small fracture to one of Nate's lower vertebrae. Although he received clearance to play in his senior year, his fear of reinjury prevented him from wholeheartedly entering into competition. Nate finished the season with the team, but it was not the ending he had hoped for.

This proved to be a defining life event for our son. He tasted disappointment for the first time and was forced to learn how to let go of a future that seemed certain.

Once again, Nate adapted. He channeled his quick reflexes and athletic ability into riding dirt bikes. After high school, he enrolled in the business degree program at the University of Winnipeg, bought a truck, and spent weekends dirt biking with friends or with his dad.

3. Nouwen, *Life of the Beloved*, 53–54.
4. Norris, *Amazing Grace*, 106.

Norm bought a dirt bike too, a powerful Honda XR 400, which was the cause of my husband's serious collarbone injury early in their adventures. Nevertheless, the two of them loved the sport, often riding the trails near the family cottage or riding with other enthusiasts in various dirt bike derbies.

Just four months before Nate's sickness, they participated in a derby in the Manitoba Sandilands Provincial Forest. When Nate got stuck in one of the many muddy stretches of the competition, Norm stopped to offer a push, only to get "roosted," or completely mud-splattered by Nate's wildly spinning back tire. The story quickly became a legend.

"Remember how I bailed you out," Norm said. "I got off my bike and waded ankle-deep into that muck to give you a push . . . and you gassed it!"

"Oh yeah," Nate said, playing along with his dad's banter. "I may have panicked . . . and you may have come a bit too close to my tail. But you told me to give'er. I was just following your instructions," he said with a silly smile.

"You know what I think?" asked Norm with a wink and a giggle. "I think you got stuck on purpose to lure me off my bike so you could get an advantage."

"Yup," Nate replied with a satisfied grin. "You found me out. That was my ploy all along!"

The story was still alive and well at Norm's fiftieth birthday during the third week of July, a month before Nate's diagnosis.

Now, the shape of this young life was forever altered; his soulscape in the throes of change.

CONVERSION IS DESCRIBED IN different ways by different Christians, depending on theological tradition. In my evangelical Anabaptist tradition, conversion is defined by a point in time, the moment of accepting Jesus Christ as personal Savior and inviting him into your heart.

I remember kneeling with my mom at my bedside at the tender age of six after attending a particularly rousing revival meeting. Convicted that I needed to be saved from my sins and saved for heaven, I followed my mom in a simple prayer. From then on, I could always point to that moment like a north star.

"I was saved when I was six," I would declare.

But what if conversion is lifelong? What if it's that moment, and so many more? This way of believing has a long history in the Christian church, beyond my Reformation roots. Sometimes it goes by a fancy theological term: sanctification.

Looking back, I see that God kept saving me again and again.

Like when I was a first-year college student, 500 miles away from home, engaging my faith as a fledgling young adult, praying my doubts. Or at nineteen, when I walked down the center aisle of my home church and said "I do" to Norm, entering into sacred union. And especially when I looked into the eyes of each of my babies for the first time.

With each seismic change, a new set of questions emerged. A new horizon with God was created, a radical reorientation toward the mystery at life's center. Always, it felt like a deeper way of knowing and being known had broken open within me. Like some invisible boundary had been pushed out to hold an even greater love.

Anglican theologian N. T. Wright calls conversion "waking up," saying that the phrase "offers one of the most basic pictures of what can happen when God takes a hand in someone's life."[5]

Waking up. It's an ancient Christian image. It's what happened in the gospel stories when Jesus raised people to life. "She's just asleep," said Jesus to the terrified parents of a dead girl in the Gospel of Luke because, in the ancient Jewish world, "sleep" was a common way of talking about death.

Waking up. It's what happened when God raised Jesus to life. The resurrection of Christ was an invitation for the world to awaken.

Waking up. It's what happens every time the "gospel of Jesus—the good news that the creator God has acted decisively to put the world to rights—impinges on someone's consciousness."[6]

For some, this waking up is a sudden and shocking experience. For others, it may happen quietly and slowly. "Most of us," says Wright, "know something of both and a lot in between."[7]

As precious as my first encounter with God was at age six, I have come to believe that "being saved" is both an event—a waking up—and a process of continual awakening. It's a shaping that occurs over a lifetime, an ever-increasing opening to God's life within.

Conversion, says Richard Rohr, is lifelong: "it happens again and again throughout our lives at ever new levels of insight."[8]

At forty-two, when I should have been settled into a profession and counting down the years to retirement, I decided to attend seminary.

A mid-life crisis? Maybe. I was a trained elementary school teacher, graduating university at age twenty-two. That same year I gave birth to our

---

5. Wright, *Simply Christian*, 205.

6. Wright, *Simply Christian*, 205.

7. Wright, *Simply Christian*, 205.

8. Rohr, "True Conversion Never Stops," lines 12–15.

first daughter, Laura. Two years later, Kate was born. And two years after that it was Nate's turn. I was a mother of three at twenty-six.

After experimenting with classroom teaching for five years after Nate entered school, I chose instead to work part-time for the church that Norm and I had started with a handful of others a few years earlier. The small congregation had grown exponentially during that period, requiring a team to staff the ever-growing children's ministry.

My job was to lead the music portion of the hour-long children's services that ran concurrently with the adult services at nine and eleven o'clock on Sunday mornings. It was rewarding work. After eight years in the position, I oversaw a group of more than forty adult volunteers. We were a community of people making a difference in the lives of children.

I spent one year leading a similar team in the adult service, but it was not the same. Something needed to change.

"Would you consider seminary?" my senior pastor asked one day.

The idea was strangely inviting and oddly persistent. But why? True, working for the church had made me a student of leadership. I read books about best practices, attended seminars and conferences, even led training sessions for churches at a national level within our denomination. Seminary would undoubtedly equip me to be a stronger leader. But there was more to it than that. Much more, as it turned out.

Helping people within a faith community invariably led to conversations about spiritual longings—ways of prayer, ways of interacting with Holy Scripture that truly satisfied. Often, what surfaced in these exchanges was a desire for more, more of God, more of what it means to be Christian. I loved this part of my job; I loved these kinds of theological conversations—they always stirred up my own desires for more of the God-life within. Was this curiosity a gift to be explored?

Books offered further clues.

"Think often of God, by day, by night, in all your pursuits and duties, even during your recreations. He is always near you and with you; do not leave him alone . . . think of Him often, adore Him continually, live and die with Him; that is the glorious business of a Christian,"[9] says Brother Lawrence, a seventeenth-century Carmelite monk in his book *Practicing the Presence of God.*

Something about this simple way of staying with God throughout the day as a way of prayer took hold in my imagination. Could prayer really be "a gentle receptiveness to divine breathings,"[10] as Thomas Kelly so

9. Brother Lawrence, *The Practice of the Presence of God*, 68.
10. Kelley, *A Testament of Devotion*, 35.

eloquently described it? This was my first foray into a more contemplative way of walking out my faith. And I wanted more.

"Some of you," Kelly says in his little book *Testament of Devotion*, "wistfully long to slip into that amazing Center where the soul is at home with God. Be very faithful to that wistful longing."[11]

I felt strangely addressed by these soulish words from this Quaker writer. In many ways, my decision to go to seminary was a response to a "wistful longing" to engage both my mind and heart in the study of God—theology.

*Ora et labora* the Christian monastics famously said—pray and work. That is what I would set out to do through my studies. Naïve? Dreamy? Maybe. Had I known the volume of writing and research that graduate studies demanded, I may have dismissed the idea outright.

But there was something else, another desire at work in me: I wanted to develop my ability to write. The desire to express myself through the written word had been planted early. It was something that seemed to come naturally and was affirmed again and again through my schooling. I had little desire to be ordained or to preach, and I had no idea what would happen afterward.

I saw this opportunity for what it was: an opening, a movement, maybe a flutter of God.

Norm was fully supportive, and our kids, with the exception of Nate, were young adults, which meant there was time and space for the rigors of graduate-level coursework. My senior pastor was delighted by my decision and helped me enroll at an interdenominational seminary nearby.

As it turned out, the building that housed the seminary was once the site of a Catholic school. The majestic bell tower that stood above the prairie landscape like a sacred sentinel provided the perfect backdrop for my midlife sabbatical.

"Fitting," I said to friends. "Part of me has always been monkish."

On the very first day, when we students sat together for orientation in one of the theaters, tears ran down my face. Yes, seminary, with its mountain of reading, research and papers, would be daunting; yes, it would ask something of me that I didn't quite know if I had. But a part of me warmed to the thought that this place was somehow a homecoming.

Three years within those seminary walls resulted in a radical shift for my Anabaptist faith. It became roomier as I reached beyond my Reformation heritage into pre-Reformation Christian thought.

---

11. Kelley, *A Testament of Devotion*, 74.

I discovered the early church Fathers like Ireneaus, Origin, and Augustine, and marveled at their tireless efforts to preserve a Trinitarian faith amid the disputes and heresies that threatened to destroy it in the first centuries after Christ. I fell in love with the creeds of the early church and whispered them with solidarity. I found a kindred spirit in Theresa of Avila, a sixteenth-century mystic who revolutionized her monastic community and wrote about her direct experience of God.

In my final year, I studied spiritual formation and became completely smitten by the spiritual practices that had shaped Christian history, learning new ways to pray using Scripture, icons, and the help of "soul friends." Through it all, I felt gathered into the great company of saints throughout the ages who deepened my identity and awareness of belonging to God.

"Stand at the crossroads and look," writes the Old Testament prophet. "Ask for the ancient paths, ask where the good way is, and walk in it, and you will find rest for your souls" (Jeremiah 6:16, NIV).

The shape of my faith was changing.

And with it, my understanding of church. Wrestling with doctrine, theology, and Scripture, and rubbing shoulders with peers and professors from diverse Christian backgrounds pushed the boundaries of the contemporary free-church culture that had shaped much of my life. Along with Robert Webber, author of *Evangelicals on the Canterbury Trail*, I would affirm that "God has his people in every expression of the faith—Catholic, Orthodox, Protestant, fundamentalist, evangelical, Holiness, charismatic."[12]

Time spent in seminary expanded my views on theological issues. My conclusion on controversial matters always came to *more*—this is *more* of the unexplainable, *more* of the indescribable, *more* at work than my enlightened mind can comprehend. Life with God, I learned, turns *more* on mystery than certainty—and mystery opens new dimensions of faith and invites new expressions of worship.

Far from shaking the foundations of my faith, this revelation felt like a homecoming for my soul, returning it to its primal state of wonder. Some new part of me was waking up. Another moment of conversion.

When I graduated in 2008, I was full of possibility, full of a new kind of confidence and belief in myself. During my three years in seminary, several professors asked if I had plans to continue my studies, to work toward an advanced master's degree, or even a PhD. My ability to write was affirmed, and when I stepped back into the world, I would answer the inevitable question "So what now?" with a chirpy certainty, "I want to write." And while I

12. Webber, *Evangelicals on the Canterbury Trail*, 64.

didn't know the specifics of such a job, I was quite sure I would recognize it when it appeared.

As it turned out, that desire did not meet with employment. In the year that followed, I volunteered at a local homeless shelter and wrote several stories about their guests for the organization's promotional brochure. But no job materialized. I did some odd assignments for my local church, but nothing that involved a paycheck.

I became discouraged and disoriented and applied for a job selling furniture. Then, in 2010, the conference job opened up—the role of writer for the national website. At last, I thought, here is the job I've been waiting for—to write news releases and stories about churches across the country and exercise my theological muscle.

Yet, six months in, I began to wonder if this was the type of writing that stirred my soul. When the question surfaced, I stuffed it down.


Now, HERE I WAS three years later journeying with a son who was in the midst of a fiery furnace of suffering, his very soul scorched by the heat. Crying out to God with desperate requests while still uttering deep gratitude in his journal, he laid it bare.

This suffering was a seminary without walls, a perilous and unbidden journey into more of the mystery of God. The roomier faith that had been formed in me through the rigors of coursework was being pressed upon, challenged at whole new level. Would it prevail?

Some nights I whispered the well-worn creed, and my heart took courage in its ancient rhythms: "I believe in the Holy Spirit, the holy catholic Church, the communion of saints, the forgiveness of sins, the resurrection of the body and life everlasting." *Yes that*, I whispered into the darkness, *yes especially that.*

And I would say it again, letting the words carry me to a place of comfort: "I believe in the resurrection of the body and life everlasting."

Although there were no degrees granted for time spent here, this experience began to radically re-shape our souls, more than a lifetime of theological education ever could. Suffering is a crucible for conversion, a summons to wake up, but it involves dying to a way of life and desperately searching the horizon for the promise of resurrection.

Most afternoons in the later weeks of September, Nate would ride shotgun in my red VW Golf, the two of us driving around the countryside as a way of passing the time. Often I practiced being a "soul friend" to my son, something I had learned about at seminary, listening to the gentle Spirit-voice within to guide our conversations.

There were the usual treks—to the provincial park, about ten square kilometers of field and trees, no more than a fifteen-minute drive from our door; or the river-road circuit, a stretch of highway north of the city following the mighty Red River as it snakes its way through miles of rural townships. And country music was the soundtrack that played in the background.

"Turn it up," Nate would say when his favorite song came on the radio. And I always obliged. The refrain of the song sounded like it belonged to that Spirit-voice—something about a blackbird and a broken wing, and the promise of flying again.

While the scenery whizzed past us, familiar and unchanged, the scenery on the inside was altogether new and constantly changing; sometimes as barren as a desert and sometimes shimmering with life.

Somewhere beneath all the brokenness was a wild notion that couldn't be tamed: sooner or later we would fly again.

# 4

# Pilgrimage

### THE THIN PLACE

My pilgrim heart comes to be
On Iona's island in the sea
Where God lingers in the majesty
Of earth and sky
And crashing shores
Vitality revealed in light and color
An invitation to draw near
Taste and see
Walk with me
Listen for your name
As gentle forces lovingly surround you
And witnesses come forward to proclaim
That the Trinity inhabiting this place
Will work in you
A beauty of the same

—JAN WOLTMANN

It was mid-September and Nate's vision began to change for the better.

Up to that point, he had been seeing double and had been experiencing a horizontal component to his condition due to complications from the tumor and hydrocephalus. When he looked out, he saw an image in multiples, up and down, left and right, which made discerning the real image a monumental challenge. The very act of focusing throughout the day left him extremely tired. Driving was out of the question for him, as the road lines were multiplied in his field of vision.

But on the third Wednesday of September, Nate noticed a shift: the horizontal images were correcting, leaving him with only double vision through his main gaze. He struggled to believe his eyes, but by Friday of that week he was completely energized by the marked improvement.

Astonishing. Another step in the miracle of restoration. Our hopes were high.

When we visited Nate's neurosurgeon, Dr. Wakefield, on September 29 for what should have been our official post-op appointment, he expressed disgust that Nate had been sent to CancerCare.

"Sorry," he said. "The system is flawed, but you were lucky to see Schneider. For a guy who looks a little burned out, he's an excellent doc."

We chuckled at the accuracy of his description. We were visibly more relaxed at this appointment, having earlier received the gist of the results.

"So, you have, as you know, an astrocytoma," he said, directing his comments to Nate.

"Invariably, lesions in this part of the brain are low-grade," he said as he leaned back in his chair, his eyes narrowing, his baritone voice commanding and oozing confidence. "Occasionally, they turn out to be high-grade—yours is not. High-grade is bad; low-grade is good," he explained, gesturing with his hands, as if comparing one brand of soft drink to another.

"So, if you look under a microscope at these things, you don't see a lot of mitotic, dividing cells, you see a little bit of hypercellularity; otherwise, it looks kind of like brain, but a bit abnormal."

This was Wakefield's classroom and we were well-behaved, attentive students.

Tall and fit, and in his mid-forties, Wakefield's manner was commanding and his tone mesmerizing. We hung on every word. Why wouldn't we? Those hands had guided a probe through the inner sanctum of our son's brain.

"Abnormal cells such as these can stay well-behaved for long stretches," he said, "but they also have the propensity to become high-grade lesions over time."

*Hmm, what exactly does that mean?* I didn't dare interrupt.

"The really important question going through your mind right now is time—how much time?"

Yes! How often that question came up on our drives . . . and how helpless I felt in the face of it. At last, we were getting some answers.

"The answer to that question is absolutely unknown for you," declared Wakefield. "I can give you a rough idea of what it is on average, but you are you, and only you count. On average, it's like ten to twelve years or more. But everybody's different. Things may change. People develop more symptoms because tumors grow; these tumors don't spread to the rest of your body, they grow locally.

"But local growth ain't great when it's right in the middle of your brain. But remember, it's conceivable that this tumor could do nothing for the next twenty years or longer."

*Did he really say twenty years or longer? That's good right?*

"Right now, there is no known treatment that can change the tumor's behavior. And there's absolutely nothing you can do to change how this is going to function in your head—no diet, no pills, no radiation."

"So that leaves you with a problem," he said, leaning back in his chair, eyes fixed on Nate. "It's a problem that's not really medical; it's existential, and I'm not a philosopher. I can't tell you how to live your life; I can tell you how you might *want* to."

We were all ears then, leaning into the wisdom offered by this superman of science.

"You need to go on with life. The worst thing you can do is surrender to this and hide in a corner, or go crazy, drop out of school, take up opium smuggling, right?"

*Wait! What? Did he really say opium smuggling?* I laughed out loud along with Nate and Norm at the prospect.

"All medicine can really answer is *What are the probabilities*? And the probabilities are that you have a long time to be Nathan, maybe a very long time."

There was something about these words and the way he uttered them that would stay with me long after this appointment, like helium when my thoughts were weighed down by doubt.

"What about radiation?" asked Norm.

"Nope," said Wakefield. "Radiation is a powerful tool for treating rapidly dividing cells in malignant tumors but completely ineffective in treating the abnormal tissue in low-grade tumors, especially those in the middle of the mid-brain."

"And surgery?" we asked.

"Bad idea," said Wakefield. "This is not a brainstem lesion that benefits from being operated on because it's at ground zero—it's at the center of everything."

Nate updated Wakefield on the status of his vision. Wakefield was enthusiastic, encouraging Nate to continue using his prism lenses and to follow through with his ophthalmologist appointment.

"How will Nate be monitored?" I asked, as our appointment neared its conclusion.

"Well," said Wakefield, "this tumor's not likely to do anything today or tomorrow or even next year. How about we do a follow-up in six months, and then a year after that?"

"An MRI is scheduled for November 1," I said, "to see how Nate's brain is settling, and to check on the ventricles."

"Even better," said Wakefield, ushering us out of the small clinic room.


To THIS DAY IT amazes me how people stumble out into the world after receiving such news. The neurosurgeon was right: science had rendered its verdict in probabilities. The implications of the diagnosis were questions of an existential nature. There was nothing more the high office of medicine could offer.

The task of grappling with the fallout and figuring out how to live was up to us. It was hard to make sense of it. It felt like we had been airdropped into another civilization, a foreign land, another planet, where we were aliens.

Somehow, without a map, we had to navigate this world, its vocabulary and customs, and create something different than we had known all our lives. Popular culture has assigned a name to this—they call it a "new normal." But this pithy phrase does not do justice to the mountain of change it represents.

Nate wrestled hard with this new reality. Would he ever find a measure of peace knowing a little mass of brain cells threatened his existence? Was peace even possible? How should he carry on? What should he do? Should he finish his schooling or choose an entirely new direction? He feared he would fail in the choosing.

At twenty-one, his way forward should have been brimming with choice and possibility, but the presence of a tumor, albeit slow-growing, had cast a long shadow.

And there were other complications, too. Despite the positive changes to his vision, reading remained a chore for his recovering brain.

Books were too overwhelming, so in the weeks following the appointment, Nate started with sports journals, featuring content with high appeal and requiring only short bursts of energy. His eyes could only properly focus when the spacing was generous; when it was not, his double vision caused him frustration and discouragement. A new kind of trepidation gripped him.

"How will I ever go back to university in the winter semester if I can't read a textbook?" he lamented on one of our drives. "How will I complete assignments if I can't read my computer screen?"

I ached for him, and grieved his innocence now receding in the distance like an object in my rearview mirror. Fear was a constant companion, as was defeat, and they came calling when he was alone.

I could hear the accusations hissing at his heart's door when his voice quivered and the tears fell. My mama-heart wanted to beat them back with memories of God's nearness, of the reminders of words and symbols that spoke of God with us.

Instead, I cried with him and raged at the broken thoughts that disrupted his peace. I wept about the chasm that separated the life he once had and the one he was now living. I wept because it was so difficult to witness his emotional pain—to touch the despair and feel helpless against it. How easily hope evaporated.

A date had been set for Kate's surgery: October 31, Halloween, the day before Nate would undergo his second MRI. Warren would perform the ligament reconstruction by doing a tissue graft—taking a healthy tendon from Kate's hamstring muscle to replace the damaged ligaments of the MCL and ACL. Recovery time would involve a rigorous commitment to physiotherapy to strengthen the muscles. It could take up to six months.

Our twenty-three-year-old had managed these weeks with a maturity beyond her years. Even though she, too, had suffered a severe injury, hobbling about the house with crutches, fiddling with her brace throughout the day and managing the ice machine that permanently sat at the foot of her bed, she had not complained that my focus had been on Nate's recovery. Her presence was a gift in this season.

The two of them, just two years apart, had been comrades since childhood, the bright and winsome Kate leading the way into adventure. Now, on most days, she joined him to watch sports shows in the late morning and the two of them would banter about the content. Nate was happy to school her on the finer points, and Kate's quick wit always found a way to entertain them both. She made him smile, even laugh out loud.

But this season was taking its toll on her, too. Her appetite had diminished significantly, and she was nauseated. Her weight loss was evident, and her energy waned. I was worried about these developments and sought help for what felt like yet another crisis in our family.

Warren arranged for some medical tests—an ultrasound to make sure there was no blockage, or abnormalities in her stomach lining. The tests came back negative. While it was true that her physical condition was fixable in the grand scheme of things, there was an emotional wound that had no quantifiable edges, nothing easily altered by a surgeon's scalpel.

The books and resources dedicated to the disequilibrium in family systems due to extreme life-crisis are legion; we were living it.

Laura and Jeff were two years married, living in an apartment only minutes away from our home. They, too, had been a gift. Jeff was the brother that Nate never had, a young professional, sharp and resourceful, with a wicked sense of humor that we had come to adore. Laura was an assistant manager at a senior's facility in the city. She possessed a lovely combination of practical wisdom and action. Her penchant for organization was exceptional.

Over the past month, Laura had taken it upon herself to monitor our many phone messages and quarterback the meals that were pouring into our home from caring friends and family. This was no small offering.

Crisis exacts a steep emotional price that renders tasks like answering phones and preparing meals difficult, if not impossible, some days. Laura stepped into this gap with ease and confidence, freeing me up to focus on the needs of Kate and Nate.

It was now the second weekend of October, Canadian Thanksgiving. The week leading up to this national holiday had been full of improvement. On Monday, Nate took my car for a few laps around the provincial park, feeling overjoyed that he could drive again. On Thursday, he started the engine of his Mazda3 for the first time in eight weeks and took it for a spin around the neighborhood. It was a monumental step in Nate's recovery, a symbol of independence he thought was gone forever.

On Sunday evening, we gathered as a family, grateful for the past seven days of abundance. The conversation around the table was lively and animated. Kate ate more than she had in two weeks. Laura and Norm were scheming to sell their opening-night NHL hockey tickets to fund a family trip to Minneapolis later in the month.

It was fall 2011, and history was being made in our city. Winnipeg was welcoming the return of the Winnipeg Jets, the professional hockey team that had been sold to Phoenix fifteen years earlier. Hockey is Canada's pastime, and this town, literally at the longitudinal center of the country, was ready to celebrate the return of their heroes with unprecedented zeal.

Opening night was less than two weeks away; tickets were worth $1,500 apiece. My husband was willing to sell both his tickets for the opportunity to be with family, eagerly putting the pair up for sale online.

Days later, Norm had a potential buyer. They agreed to meet at a nearby Starbucks for the exchange, with Laura along for the ride.

But when he walked into the cafe, Norm was blindsided. It was a setup. The potential buyer turned out to be an undercover officer and Norm ended up in the back seat of an unmarked police car. The officer confiscated the tickets and began to write Norm a hefty fine.

Laura called me to come quickly. At first, I didn't believe her, chiding her for a prank I was sure her father had concocted.

After all, we had joked about this very scenario at the supper table. We knew that the Jets franchise, in response to unregulated online ticket sales, had just set up a ticket-selling agency of their own, making it illegal to sell tickets privately.

As I pulled up alongside the unmarked police car, I connected with Norm's anxious eyes in the back seat and felt my indignation rise. This man to whom I'd pledged my one and only life was steadfast and strong, a hero and warrior in his own right. I was suddenly overcome by renewed love and respect for him, fierce in my defense of his actions, despite their legal implications.

One of the police officers, the younger of the two, got in my vehicle and rehearsed the charges. I exploded into a fever-pitched explanation, recounting our story and the reason we were selling the tickets in the first place, coming at him with all the intensity of a cornered mama bear.

Eyes down, fingers fumbling with the papers in his hands, the young officer stayed silent, looking sheepish, like a scolded schoolboy.

"I'm sorry ma'am," he said in a small voice, even though he was unable to waive the fine.

It would be years before we found the humor in that story.

The mood that pulsed through the city, upbeat and expectant, registered only dissonance in me. Any other year, I would have been swept up in the hockey celebration. But this year was so very different.

Shadowed by suffering, our focus had shifted. What used to satisfy—entertainment, shopping, restaurant-going—no longer did.

Instead, we were learning to live with new expectations, altered life expectancy and a great deal of ambiguity in this after-land. The pleasure of sharing time with our beloveds was paramount, even if it landed us on the wrong side of the law for a day.

For all the hairpin twists and turns in our pilgrim journey, mercy, like the mighty Red we followed most days, flowed alongside us with equal intensity. On one unusually hot day in late October, we drove the distance to River Road.

It was a glorious morning; the fall air was crisp but not cold, the sky overhead an endless blue. It was the kind of morning that opened our hearts to hope, to hear and notice the many and varied ways that God was speaking the same refrain: "I am your God and will take care of you until you are old and your hair is grey. I made you and will care for you; I will give you help and rescue you" (Isaiah 46:4, GNB). How often in these weeks had Nate heard a version of this message from so many sources unconnected by time or place?

"I will take care of you," God was saying to my son. On that morning, Nate had a clear sense that he need not fear the future, finishing school or finding work, a life-partner, or a place to live. Those would be provided.

*Gotcha.* That word which God fastened to Nate's heart as his life unraveled now found deeper meaning.

On that pristine morning, we sat at a picnic table overlooking the river. Nate went back to his experience of God after surgery, the days he had spent recovering on the couch with his eyes closed against the pain and fatigue within his body. A cocoon of darkness.

As he talked, he positioned his arms as if holding a newborn, illustrating exactly how God had held him.

"I felt cradled," he said in hushed tones, still astonished by the memory. "I've never experienced such peace, love, and contentment in life. I didn't know it was possible."

It was a window into a profound experience. For my son, the experience was otherworldly, so much so that he struggled for vocabulary to describe the feeling, the knowing.

"Most of us arrive at a sense of self and vocation only after a long journey through alien lands," says Parker Palmer in his book titled *Let Your Life Speak.* "But this journey bears no resemblance to the trouble-free 'travel packages' sold by the tourism industry. It is more akin to the ancient tradition of pilgrimage—'a transformative journey to a sacred center' full of hardships, darkness, and peril."[1]

> In the tradition of pilgrimage, those hardships are seen not as accidental but as integral the journey itself. Treacherous terrain,

---

1. Palmer, *Let Your Life Speak,* 17–18.

bad weather, taking a fall, getting lost—challenges of that sort, largely beyond our control, can strip the ego of the illusion that it is in charge and make space for the true self to emerge. If that happens, the pilgrim has a better chance to find the sacred center he or she seeks. Disabused of our illusions by much travel and travail, we awaken one day to find that the sacred center is here and now—in every moment of the journey, everywhere in the world around us, and deep within our own hearts.[2]

In the years to come, I would travel to the distant island of Iona, Scotland, as part of a pilgrimage. It is said that Iona is a *thin* place on the planet, a place where heaven and earth mingle such that God's presence is palpable. My pilgrim heart would recognize it, too, when I landed on the shores of that little patch of earth nestled in the ocean—God showing off every square inch of his majesty in shades of green and blue.

How could an island three miles long and one mile wide revolutionize Christian history? God only knows.

And those high Celtic crosses reaching to heaven. They would invite me to come near and listen; to perhaps hear my own name among the saints—all those monks and nuns, artists, scribes, and scholars whose footprints were buried ten centuries deep. All proclaiming that the Trinity inhabiting this place would work in me a beauty of the same.

Perhaps that is why I would agree to travel all those miles, just to see, touch, participate in the land's long history of glory. And to let it claim me.

Yet, one need not journey to the far corners of the globe to be a pilgrim. Suffering, too, sets the soul on a pilgrimage through alien lands, stripping the ego of the illusion that it is in charge, making space for the self that it was born to be. Suffering is a *thin* place where God's presence oddly shimmers through darkness and peril. This is a mystery and a mercy too great for human understanding. Holy ground. The heart's long history of glory waiting to be claimed.

I perceived it then, even as I listened to Nate's divine encounter in the arms of the Almighty, his "sacred center" in the midst of travail. Perhaps, in the ancient tradition of Christian pilgrimage, geographical coordinates are of less consequence than the spiritual coordinates which orient the soul to God, deep within the heart.

IT IS NOW THE first week of November. Nate has had his first follow-up MRI. Kate is recovering from knee surgery.

---

2. Palmer, *Let Your Life Speak*, 18.

On Sunday, November 6, Nate shares his story with our church via a video clip that was made toward the end of October. In it, he speaks of his experiences of God's presence alongside the lived fears of his diagnosis. He shares news of the pathology results and expresses his thanksgiving.

Meanwhile, I am asking people on our e-mail distribution list—which has grown considerably larger over the last twelve weeks—to pray that this MRI will reveal a dramatic change in the tumor, a complete disappearance or sizeable shrinkage.

"Lord Jesus," I pray, "you are in charge, overseeing this process. All cells are ordered by you, and in you is life. So, we believe that you will do what is best for us, and that your way will be the better way. But, oh God, we dare to hope that you do the miraculous and touch our boy's brain with your healing hand. Astonish our doctors and confound the medical community with the revelation of your glory and majesty."

But that same week, something disconcerting happens. We are once again summoned by CancerCare for an appointment to hear the MRI results. Surely this is another mistake, a glitch in the system.

When I try to contact Dr. Wakefield's office for clarification, we are given the message that he has not yet received the report. The back-and-forth communication leaves us edgy and panicked.

Finally, it is determined that we will hear the results through our neurosurgeon, Dr. Wakefield, at his office on Thursday, November 10.

This time, our already fragile world will break into a million pieces.

# 5

## Descent

### WOMB OF GOD

What shall we say about this dark night of soul
Which banishes the light of life's frail certainties
And casts us into deep shadows?
Could this night be the womb of eternal God?
Holding us, then, beneath the heartbeat of the universe,
Encased in loving presence, nourished by a cord of mercy.
Though our doubts and fears kick and thrash against it,
The womb holds us fast;
Protected and hidden,
Preserved from the terror
In ways unseen.
Who will announce that the darkness in which we swim
Shall soon birth us into new life?

—JAN WOLTMANN

ON THURSDAY AFTERNOON IN mid-November, we had a meeting to hear the results of the MRI. It was supposed to be a routine scan after surgery to check the success of the ventriculostomy and take measurements of the slow-growing tumor. We had seen Dr. Wakefield just six weeks earlier to hear the results of the biopsy, and he had indicated this would be the first of many such checkups at three-month intervals.

Still, we were praying for a miracle—to hear news that the tumor had somehow disappeared or shrunk considerably.

As we settled into the waiting room of the neurosurgery unit, we watched patients disappear into the clinic rooms, bantering about what to eat for supper. Nate sat between Norm and I, dressed in the same white T-shirt he had worn when he was admitted to the hospital for surgery. It was his lucky T-shirt, reminding him of all that had been accomplished in his story.

An hour later, at four o'clock, when Nate's name was finally called, the waiting room was almost empty. Our appointment was saved for last.

When we entered the room, we found Dr. Wakefield seated at his desk, seemingly absorbed by his screen, as per usual, scrolling through what appeared to be Nate's file on his computer. His back was turned as we took our seats.

Nate sat on the examination table, feet dangling just above the floor. Norm took a seat next to him and I sat on the chair closest to the doctor so I could record the meeting.

Silence.

A full minute and a half passed before Wakefield said a word.

"So, your scans are back," he said, his eyes glued to the images on his computer screen.

"And I gotta tell you one thing." His tone was flat, almost accusatory. "The results don't make me happy."

More silence followed as Wakefield scrolled between images. The shape of Nate's skull came into three-dimensional view from several vantage points, along with the cloudy mass of cells at the base of his brainstem. It was the second time we had seen these pictures. The first was when Nate was diagnosed in the middle of August. Then, as now, the images traveled straight to my gut producing a sickening sense of panic.

"I don't know if you can see from there," he said in Nate's direction, "but these are the two pictures that interest me the most. Let me see if I can make them bigger."

As Wakefield fiddled with his program, the only sounds in that stark little room were the clicking of a computer mouse and several deep sighs from Nate. This continued for four agonizing minutes. *Why couldn't Wakefield just say it?*

Gone was the neurosurgeon who had greeted us warmly at our last appointment to tell us face-to-face about the good news of the pathology report. Gone was the doctor who had encouraged our son about the existential nature of his journey, suggesting that Nate, in all probability, had a long time to be Nate in this world. Gone was any hint of joviality.

Gone, in a word, was hope.

"On most of these images, the tumor seems slightly larger by two to three millimeters, which we shouldn't be seeing in a low-grade lesion. That suggests this is somewhat of a higher-grade problem than pathology indicated."

The cursor was now directly on the mass, as Dr. Wakefield attempted to measure it by adjusting his computer mouse. All the while he faced the screen, talking and analyzing the images as I imagined he might do with his medical team. We were a full seven minutes into the meeting. My mouth was dry and sickness rose in my gut.

I looked over at Norm, his face ashen. Nate's eyes registered only confusion and shock. All of us were speechless, tangled in the clinical analysis of those awful pictures, held captive to a computer screen that glowered with multiple images of Nate's skull. Each image bore the dreadful cloud of cells our neurosurgeon was desperately trying to measure. Agonizing minutes passed.

"This sequence here," he said, pointing to another set of images, "suggests that it's a little bigger than it was before. Not by much, maybe 10 percent in diameter, but that's significant."

*These can't be Nate's scans. Dear God, no! This nightmare of a report must be a mistake. This is completely absurd. Please God, no. Breathe.*

"So, when the pathology report said there was no multiplication of cells," I finally blurted, giving voice to my doubts and growing anxiety, "that wasn't true?"

"Well," said Wakefield carefully, turning in his chair for the first time to face me. "Imagine you have an apple with a few big bruises on it. And all you do is take a couple small nibbles of the apple, the only part you can see. That taste tells you either the apple is very bruised, or perhaps, it's quite normal. But a nibble can't tell you about the apple as a whole. Tumors are exactly like that. Tumors can have areas that are in the normal range, and areas that are highly abnormal."

"So, there are areas of abnormality?" I asked, wincing at the analogy of an apple representing my son's brain, unable to fully process the doctor's words, my mind a crash site of information and shock.

In response, Wakefield launched into an explanation about the nature of pathology, concluding that the sample that had been taken was small and incomplete. Pathology could successfully determine the type of tumor—in this case, one that was of astrocytic origin—but that it could only represent the sample and not the tumor as a whole.

Wakefield pointed back to the screen, reiterating that these images were now the best indicator of how the tumor was behaving.

"And it's aggressive," he repeated.

"Which means . . . ?" my voice small and thin and trailing into the abyss of these ugly words.

"Which means it's appropriate to apply treatments that we would use for more aggressive brain tumors in this lineage of glial cells—by administering oral chemotherapy and radiotherapy."

Cancer.

"So, back to Dr. Schneider then?" I asked in a voice not my own, as if someone had drained all emotion from my words. Something fierce in me wanted to exit the room, to somehow un-hear this horrific conversation. Nate and Norm remained speechless. The room was too small for the heartache that was building.

"Yes, it's back to Dr. Schneider and the brain tumor clinic.

"They do Friday meetings," continued Wakefield, "so they'll see you next Friday. And we'll re-think what to do. The strategies are pretty standard, and the clinic has all the mechanisms for putting those treatments into play. What I don't think needs to happen is more surgery because this isn't operable given the surrounding, healthy brain tissue. And you can't go in *there* for obvious reasons."

More words filled the room while our faces drained of color. How we managed to stay in our seats and will ourselves to listen to this suffocating news remains a mystery to me. Shock, I suppose. Perhaps some level of disassociation occurs, a shutoff valve triggered when our emotional circuits are overwhelmed. I don't know for sure.

What I do know is that it would be years before I could listen to the recording of this meeting, and even then, the emotional impact was like a swift blow to the gut.

"The game plan needs to change when the facts change," Wakefield said.

"Okay," I responded, and Norm echoed a mechanical, "Okay."

It was now fifteen minutes into the meeting.

"Could Nate have any additional symptoms as a result of the change?" I asked, suddenly afraid of what this meant for life outside these walls. Would his vision change again? Could he go blind, or worse, could this growing tumor cause him to lose control of his motor movements, a kind of stroke paralyzing parts of his body or face? Could he seizure?

"Everything from a coma to nothing," Wakefield said, his tone matter-of-fact.

More was said after that, but my mind could not register any of it. The word "coma" was coming at me like a bat out of hell, threatening my very sanity. That word, and all the ones in between, from stroke to seizure, would be the reason I hesitated to leave the house. And when I did go for a walk or leave to get some groceries, I would panic whenever I heard the sound of distant sirens, sure they had been called to our home.

"That's not the news we wanted to hear today," I muttered in spite of myself.

What I really wanted to do was scream, long and loud. *No! You're wrong! This is all a mistake!* I wanted to throw myself headlong into that computer screen. I wanted to cut every wire and smash it into a thousand bits. I wanted to pick up whatever shred of life was left in that room and tell that neurosurgeon in no uncertain terms that we quit; that we were done with MRIs, with measurements, with explanations, with next steps.

"It's not the conversation any of us wanted to have," said Wakefield in a gentle tone, his facial expression softening a little.

Surely he had drawn the short straw among his colleagues. Who wants to share such news with another human being? Science may be able to describe and explain the facts, but it is far too small to bear the full weight of such a diagnosis. Something greater than science must come to our rescue then.

"There's no question this is not good. But what *is* good is that we have the evidence in hand to begin the hard work of treating it," he said in the most convincing tone he could muster.

"That's all you can do, I guess," said Nate, speaking for the first time, his voice trembling and timid, suggesting that tears were forming in great pools around his heart.

"I wish I could think of something else to say, or had something else to say, but I don't," said Wakefield, looking directly at Nate. "We have to kick it up a notch." And with that, he stood up to leave.

But before he did, he firmly touched Nate's shoulder and spoke a heartfelt promise, "We've got your back, okay!"

We would remember those words and carry them with us into the dark night of treatment, although I doubt Wakefield knew their power and the kernel of mercy hidden within them. For in those words, we heard the very voice of God conspiring for our good, a holy collaboration between a group of physicians and the Great Physician.

"We've got your back" came to mean that God was in—and through and above—the science.

The whole exchange took less than twenty minutes.

In that span of time, the precarious path we had journeyed for the past three months was destroyed with nuclear force.

Gone was the joy we had experienced during our recent five-kilometer bike ride and the restoration of physical stamina it represented for our son. Gone was the euphoria we witnessed as Nate took his rightful place behind the wheel of his Mazda3 after his vision had returned.

All the hard-fought hope we had gathered with the greatest of care over the past weeks incinerated in that clinic room until all that was left were ashes, swirling around our feet as we walked into the night.

THE TEARS THAT HAD been gathering roll freely on the long, silent drive home.

Kate greets us cheerfully as we walk in the front door. She has baked chocolate cupcakes to celebrate what we all thought would be an encouraging appointment. Nate is sobbing now, his grief coming quickly in great gasps.

"I don't want to die," Nate repeats again and again, with a guttural anguish that threatens his breathing and convulses his body. We sit beside him on our living room couch while he rocks back and forth.

I am undone, dreadfully afraid this kind of intense reaction will trigger something terrible. "Coma," the word comes at me again, only this time, its ugliness has lodged itself in my heart. I grab some Ativan from the bathroom, hoping to calm Nate down with a tablet. But he pushes it away.

"I need to feel this pain," he cries repeatedly between great sobs.

The moment demolishes us in ways unutterable. The emotional pain he speaks of, which moves erratically through his being, is far too great for such small shoulders. We form a shield around him once again, Norm holding his shuddering frame with his big arms. I am on my knees in front of him, holding his hands in mine, pleading the only truth I know: "You are here, Nate, you are here. Please breathe. Look into my eyes. Repeat after me, 'I am here.'"

Eventually, a stillness settles over him, if only temporarily.

We are free falling into darkness. Pain slices our chests wide open and grief spills out into every conversation from that hour forward.

"The tumor is growing. Our hearts are broken," is the message we send to the community.

On this night, no winged creature appears, no butterfly announces God's nearness to bring comfort to all that trembles within us. On this night, no new word of divine consolation arrives to quell our doubts and fears. On this night, desolation is our only companion.

We drown in our tears and dare to speak aloud our disappointment with God. We name his absence. There is no food or sleep in this abyss.

"No one chooses the dark night; the dark night descends," says Barbara Brown Taylor. "When it does, the reality that troubles the soul most is the apparent absence of God. If God is light, then God is gone. There is no soft glowing space of safety in this dark night. There is no comforting sound coming out of it, reassuring the soul that all will be well."[1]

Tonight, we are beyond mercy's reach.

---

1. Taylor, *Learning to Walk in the Dark*, 134.

# 6

## Darkness

O you guiding night!
O night more lovely than the dawn!
O night that has united
the Lover with his beloved,
transforming the beloved in her Lover.

—St. John of the Cross


CHRISTIAN TRADITION IS WELL acquainted with a darkness of spirit where, in the words of Joan Chittister, "all the things we depended on to keep us safe, to show us the way, to give us reason for going on, disappear."[1] The foremost master of this night is St. John of the Cross, a sixteenth-century monk who began his renowned work, *Dark Night of the Soul*, which included a poem and two extensive commentaries about the poem, during the eleven months he spent in a monastery prison.

John was a reformer from Spain, part of the Counter-Reformation— or Catholic Reformation—which was ignited in response to the Protestant movement taking Europe by storm. Because of the seismic changes the Protestant Reformation brought to Christianity, many people often overlook the fact that the Roman Catholic Church underwent a radical revival of its own during this time in history.

1. Chittister, *Scarred By Struggle*, 38.

A Roman Catholic priest in the Carmelite order, John participated in this internal fight for reform at the invitation of his good friend St. Teresa of Avila, a Carmelite nun. Together they implemented changes to the order that resulted in significant growth and renewal for the community.

However, like those of their Protestant counterparts, John and Teresa's reforms posed a threat to the religious establishment of the day. In 1577, John was imprisoned by those within the Carmelite order who opposed his changes. While in the monastery jail, he endured regular lashings before the community and was kept in a cell barely large enough for his body. He was not allowed to bathe or change his clothes, and survived on little more than bread and water.

Barbara Brown Taylor summarizes the story this way:

> After two months, John was placed in solitary confinement, where the only light he saw came through a slit in his prison wall. It was there that he began to compose his greatest works, first by memorizing the words in the dark and later, thanks to a kind jailer, by writing them down. When he escaped after nine months, he fled to the south of Spain, where the reformed Carmelites were freer from persecution. There he continued to write down what he had learned in the dark . . . Contrary to what one might think, *Dark Night of the Soul* does not recount the horrors of John's prison experience and the faith he found there. In fact, John's night does not have much to say about religion at all. Rather, his language is passionate and speaks directly to the senses. For him, the dark night is a love story, full of the painful joy of seeking the most elusive lover of all.[2]

Had St. John of the Cross been my companion that Thursday night in November, he would have assured me that this darkness, this great unknown, was not what it seemed—it was not sinister or evil but a place of great mystery, profoundly sacred and precious. He may even have suggested that it was an opening, a portal for a deeper way of knowing and being known—a place of profound transformation, a chrysalis.

Though such comments would seem incompatible with my grief and despair, I imagine the sixteenth-century saint would have been undeterred by the emotional force within me. Instead, he would have offered a tender gaze and kindly silence amidst my protests. And when I had exhausted myself into stillness, he would have spoken gently with all the wisdom of a soul warmed by the compassion of Christ himself.

---

2. Taylor, *Learning to Walk in the Dark*, 137.

"That emptiness you are experiencing," he would say slowly, "that loss of all you hold dear will rip a crater in your soul that must be filled. Into this void, God's love will rush in, pure and holy, full of mercy.

"You don't perceive it now," he would continue. "How can you? Your soul feels so very lost to what it once knew, what it once trusted. Now, God must take you by the hand and guide you in this darkness, as though you were blind, along a way and to a place you know not, a place you never would have reached on your own.[3]

"But fear not," he would whisper, "in this place of unknowing, you will become vulnerable to God's protection, he will pull you close and keep you safe, and transform this darkness into a guiding night, *a night more lovely than the dawn.*"[4]

For St. John of the Cross, *la noche oscura del alma*, the dark night of the soul, was "something mysterious and unknown, profoundly sacred and precious beyond all imagining."[5]

In my mind's eye, I could see them, one by one, the ancients, the Old Testament saints who had endured the dark night.

There was Jacob, a bit of a scoundrel according to the Genesis account, fighting with a man, presumably an angel or God himself, wrestling all night for a blessing. And though Jacob would receive his blessing in the morning, he would bear the wound of that encounter and walk with a limp for the rest of his days.

Job, too, came into view. A saintly man, severely tested by the loss of all he held dear, arguing, wrestling, demanding that God show himself and defend his purpose for this dark night of Job's existence. And God did show himself, in a way Job did not expect, and God blessed Job with more abundance than he could hold.

And who could forget Abraham, asked by God to walk up the mountain with his young son, Isaac, and sacrifice him. In the end, God pulled back the dagger, and father and son walked back home together. God commended Abraham's faith and he became the father of an entire nation. Yet, what kind of gaping place did that experience leave inside Abraham's father-heart?

And then I saw Jesus. Bent over and alone in a garden. Praying to his Father. His grief pooling in blood and tears before the hour of his crucifixion, his body shaking. Where was God on that dark night? Was he absent? Or was he hanging on the cross, bearing our griefs and sorrows, together with his only begotten Son. Love come down.

---

3. St. John of the Cross, *The Collected Works*, 432.
4. St. John of the Cross, *The Collected Works*, 359.
5. May, *The Dark Night of the Soul*, 67.

Where was God on that dark night? His grief was rumbling, covering the earth in a shroud of darkness. Rupturing the ground and resurrecting the saints. Ripping the veil in his temple in great lament, showing the world the gaping place in his heart and inviting us in.

For God so loved the world, says the apostle John. Where was God on the world's darkest, most bleak of nights? He was there, bearing, forgiving, grieving, guiding—and three days later, resurrecting. Raising Jesus from death to life and, with him, the whole world.

The darkness could not overcome such light.

Maybe it was true, what St. John of the Cross was saying. Maybe he was right—that the darkness would become for me a guiding night. I could only hope that I, too, would come out the other side into the light; my wounds, the portal for blessings; my deaths, a resurrection.

"You will see," the sage of suffering would whisper. "Your experience of this dark night will give its gifts, leaving you freer than you were before, more available to God, more responsive to his ways, and more grateful. But these gifts won't arrive until the darkness passes. They will only come with the dawn.[6]

"Hush now," the saintly man would tenderly say. "Let us not be too quick to talk about the dawn, for it is not here yet. Just remain conscious. If you can stay with this moment in which God seems most absent, the night will do the rest.[7] I will bear this grief and sorrow with you until you can see some light."

It was days before we could say the word "cancer" out loud.

When my dad asked, "Does the growth of the tumor mean it's cancer?" the word crashed through my consciousness. Still, I struggled to grasp it.

Dr. Wakefield had not said it directly. Instead he used words like "growing," "high grade," and "abnormalities" to announce the dreaded disease.

"A tureen of tragedy is best allotted by the spoonful,"[8] says neurosurgeon Paul Kalanithi in his book, When Breath Becomes Air.

We can only bear so much darkness. We can only ingest little bits at a time because the whole of it would surely consume our sanity. Norm and I had just barely accepted the news that a small mass of slow-growing cells would forever change the trajectory of our son's future, doling out life in years, rather than decades.

6. May, The Dark Night of the Soul, 3.

7. Taylor, Learning to Walk in the Dark, 146.

8. Kalanithi, When Breath Becomes Air, 94.

By admitting this was brain cancer, those years might crush into months. Letting go of the bad for the worse was excruciating.

The sadness collecting within Nate became unbearable to witness in the days leading up to the appointment at CancerCare. Our daily drives around the countryside were now full of tears: tears for the adult he would never become; tears for the loved ones he would leave behind; tears for all the uncertainty of how death would come.

"No one can tell me it will be okay," he cried with disbelieving insistence. My soul was crushed beneath his statement. For surely this is the greatest gift a mother-heart can offer through all the scrapes and bruises of life—to wrap herself around her young and say tenderly, "All will be well. The crisis will pass, and you will survive." To be denied this sacred right of maternal love, to be forced to stand silent before impending calamity and suffer death alongside a child is the greatest grief of all.

Then a surprising thing happened. A way opened in the darkness. And my wise husband immediately recognized it as the only way forward.

He would tell me about the exchange that evening. It happened on a late afternoon drive down River Road, when he and Nate were parked in a spot overlooking the river as darkness descended over the icy waters.

"A silence hung between us like thick fog," Norm explained, "and I could barely speak.

"'I have to let you go,' I told him. 'You weren't mine to begin with. You were given to me for a time. You belong to God.

"'If I want to have any hope of living these days well, I have to let go of what I can't control. And I can't control what's going to happen to you.'"

Now my own face was wet with tears. I imagined my husband in the cab of the truck, releasing these words into the evening air. I was so proud of him, of his courage to confront the appalling darkness with the naked truth of what the darkness demanded: to let go; to hand over the life of his boy, his best friend on earth.

"As always in the precious process of the night," says May, "the divine liberation takes place in ways that are obscure to us. Sometimes we may experience it as an inner relaxation and letting go. At other times, it may feel like something we cling to is being ripped away from us. Either way, the freedom comes only through relinquishment."[9]

"What happened next?" I asked softly. "How did Nate respond?"

"He broke down" Norm said. "He told me he wasn't afraid to die, that he had even been given a measure of peace about it. 'I don't want to leave you,' he kept repeating between sobs. 'I don't want to leave my family.'"

---

9. May, *The Dark Night of the Soul*, 87.

Norm looked at me, reaching for the words, "He told me what he feared most was hurting us—hurting you and me."

We were both crying now. Our son was thinking more about us than himself in his moment of grief. I had heard bits of Nate's heartache, but there it was laid bare. "And what did you say?"

"We talked about how his Oma was gone, but that we had adjusted," said Norm, when his voice steadied. I nodded, remembering how difficult it was to lose Norm's mom. And when I looked over, I could see that a deep ache made it difficult for my husband to formulate the words, to relive his conversation with our son.

"I told him he didn't need to worry about us, that we would somehow move through our pain, that we would hurt but would go on without him."

Silence.

I had always known my husband possessed a wisdom that cut through to the truth when it mattered. I had experienced it often in our marriage, during our disagreements, when our egos both dug in and he would bring us back with a gentle word.

But this kind of wisdom, born out of the worst kind of paternal pain, was beyond anything I could have imagined. Norm's father-heart knew what his son needed in order to live through the present terror: the permission to let go. In a profound act of sacrificial love, Norm allowed his son to unburden himself of the weight that his loss would leave behind.

At that moment, Nate was able to relinquish his young life, still pregnant with unfulfilled dreams, and release himself into the arms of his Heavenly Father.

That same week, we gathered with Norm's extended family to pray. This time, we met in a house that belonged to the church where Norm's sister, Marlene, and her family attended. The little bungalow, located steps away from the church building, was set apart as a place for congregants to pray twenty-four hours a day, seven days a week.

They named it the "prayer furnace" because, for the past eleven years, not a single day or night had gone by without someone praying within its walls. Marlene had spent many an hour in that house praying for Nate since his diagnosis. That afternoon, she had reserved it for a two-hour timeslot.

There were almost twenty of Nate's aunts, uncles, and cousins in attendance. They sat in solidarity with us in this place set apart for conversation with God. That alone held holy comfort for me as I looked from person to person in this strange sanctuary.

Nate's uncle Gary spoke first.

"How are you Nate?" he asked gently. Gary was Norm's brother-in-law, married to Norm's sister. A burly sort of man, bearded, rough on the exterior, Gary had been a farmer for most of his life, able to build houses and fix anything. He laughed long and loud at family gatherings and was on the receiving end of many disapproving glances for disrupting the good German order of things.

But his interior was full of tenderness and he loved God and could see into the realm of God's world in ways akin to prophets of old.

"I'm disappointed with God," Nate replied with honest emotion. "The doctor's words blindsided me, and I feel hurt and betrayed." Silence. "But I am starting to believe in him again, and what I keep hearing is, 'There's so much more for you.'"

Nate was positioned in the middle of the circle as the family came close. Some were on their knees around him, while others stood. All reached out to him in our familiar way of prayer. Nate's Opa prayed for wisdom for us and for the doctors as they plotted the way forward.

Then Gary prayed. But his words quickly turned to groaning and he began to weep. Deep guttural sounds came from the very core of his being. It was the sound of a thousand sorrows crying our collective tears. And it broke open a well of anguish within me: tears of sadness, frustration, and anger. Tears of lament.

Afterward, a man came into view at the edge of the crowded living room. He looked to be in his late thirties, his skin black as night, eyes bright and alert, scanning our diverse crew. His five-foot-eight frame was pacing the back of the room, a black, leather-bound Bible in hand. He had booked the next time slot and was patiently waiting for us to finish.

Marlene beckoned to him. She introduced him as Henry, a Liberian native who, before he had moved to Canada a year earlier, had been a pastor in Nigeria. After offering a brief overview of our story, Marlene asked Henry to pray for Nate.

Henry didn't hesitate to enter our circle. At first he prayed in hushed tones, reflecting a deep reverence and humility before the Almighty. I heard him repeatedly say the words "your son," stirring a sense of reassurance within me. Yes, Nate was my son. But what's more, Nate was God's beloved son. I was strangely comforted to know I could only carry this boy so far as a mother. It was God's responsibility to carry him on the further journey.

Then Henry moved closer to Nate and placed his hands on his head. Suddenly, Henry's voice became fierce.

"Out!" he cried, his words shaking the very foundations of that little room. "Anything that doesn't belong in this holy temple, get *out*!" His voice reverberated through the room and thundered in our chests.

Dear God! Never had I heard this kind of prayer. It made the hair on the back of my neck stand on end. Yet, oddly, it didn't frighten me. This Liberian man, unacquainted with Canadian politeness, roared with a righteous anger, jealous for what was most precious.

Here was someone who expressed anger and disgust with the injustice of this illness. Here was someone who tore open the veil of our despair and stood boldly before the Holy of Holies. Henry's way of praying, I would learn, was born out of the African night, where dark forces are recognized and repeatedly confronted by unspeakable light. And the forces flee.

"Do you see it?" I could hear St. John of the Cross whisper. "There, in the secret places of the earth's deep darkness. There, in the passionate prayer of this mysterious stranger. It may seem dim, but it's a sliver of dawn. Into your night a light is shining. Take heart."

# 7

# Initiation

Radiation therapy is common for brain tumour patients. Radiation is directed at the patient's tumour to control or shrink whatever amount of tumour is present. This treatment is often used for malignant brain tumours . . .

—Brain Tumour Patient Resource Handbook[1]

"So, Wakefield is really pushing to treat this aggressively. And I think he's right," Dr. Schneider announced when he entered the room, without so much as a "hello."

His tone was serious and authoritative, but his appearance was still casual and rumpled.

"There's much more inflammation in the latest scan and the tumor appears to be invading the brainstem."

It was Friday, November 18, and the three of us were again face-to-face with the peculiar oncologist with a deep, raspy voice, specializing in radiotherapy to fight cancer in its most lethal form. Although his appearance was comical and bumbling, he was a true professional, possessing an incredible amount of wisdom and dedication. All we had to do was look into his eyes to see it.

We had entered the world of CancerCare for the second time in ten weeks. This time, we would not be dismissed as a glitch in the system, an

1. Brain Tumour Foundation of Canada, *Brain Tumour Handbook*, 83.

administrative error in the hasty processing of brain tumor patients. Gone was our blissful ignorance about this place.

This time, we walked into the foreboding building fully aware and full of questions after the initial shock of the cancer diagnosis. This time, we were ready with a full page of queries and a recorder in hand to confront the details of our plight.

"So it's *definitely not* a low-grade tumor anymore?" I asked. Maybe by some small miracle Wakefield's assessment was wrong. Maybe the spread was the result of the tumor having more space to expand? Maybe . . . no, not at all likely. Wildly wishful, in fact.

"It certainly doesn't look low-grade at all," he said, eyes locked on us from underneath those unruly eyebrows, his tone firm but compassionate. "Not with that much growth. If it had been a standard low-grade tectal glioma, there wouldn't have been any growth. We would have relaxed a bit and conducted scans at regular intervals. Those can go for years without growing."

"And the biopsy that showed no cancer just means they got part of it?" Norm asked, reiterating our earlier conversation with Dr. Wakefield, the sadness in his voice laced with regret, maybe skepticism.

How often had we rehearsed and scrutinized our conversation with the neurosurgeon. How often had other people raised our doubts about the contradictory results of the biopsy versus the MRI. How had the story changed so quickly?

"Unfortunately, yes," said Schneider, pausing to look directly at Norm.

"Unlike a tumor in the frontal lobe, where a large chunk can be removed for testing and slides, this biopsy was small; four pieces, each the size of a grain of rice, and justifiably so—we can only safely take needle bits from the brainstem. It was a very small sample of a relatively large mass."

"Keep in mind these things can be very heterogeneous," Schneider said, "meaning the cells are very different in different areas of the tumor. A breast tumor or a lung tumor, by contrast, is usually homogenous—if it's high-grade in one area, it's high-grade throughout.

"But the brain isn't like that," he continued. "You can have one area that's very aggressive and one area that isn't. And if you happen to put the needle into the area where it's not aggressive, well . . . you can't be sure it's an accurate representation of the whole. Does that make sense?"

We nodded. In truth, we were completely clueless, though the image of the apple made an unwelcome reappearance in my mind.

The brain tumor road is never straightforward. The whole thing is fraught with twists and turns, always changing, only able to offer science's best guess at the moment.

This much was clear: information was being shared with us on a need-to-know basis. Ten weeks ago, we had no knowledge that brain tumors differed from tumors elsewhere in the body—that these things were either heterogeneous or homogeneous. And what if we had? What then? To this day, I'm thankful we resisted opening our soul to the internet.

"It sounds like there's been consultation," I said. "You indicated Wakefield consulted with others?"

"Let me tell you something," said Schneider, his body leaning into the conversation, his tone serious, like he was letting us in on a secret.

"Wakefield called me to his office last Monday and we looked at the scans together, side by side. Then he consulted with the radiologist to make sure everyone agreed with the results. He was exceptionally thorough and cautious," Schneider said.

A sudden smirk played at the edge of his lips as he recounted the exchange. "Wakefield is very self-confident, if you know what I mean . . . like when he says something, it's like the word of God."

We all smiled a wee bit then, picturing these two men, so very different in their appearance and demeanor, the neurosurgeon-would-be-king paired with quirky oncologist who seemed better suited to the role of court jester or mad scientist. This burst of insight brought a bit of humanity into the room.

It was also clear that Wakefield wasn't kidding when he said he had Nate's back. He had been busy gathering people around Nate's results. That was comforting.

"With any kind of high-grade astrocytoma," explained Schneider, "we recommend a combination of radiation treatments with a chemotherapy drug called temozolomide, which works in addition to the radiation to attack the tumor."

"Temozolomide is taken in pill form at a dosage of 75 milligrams, seven days a week throughout the course of treatment," he said. "Afterwards, we increase it to 150 milligrams. While it causes the usual nausea and constipation, which we can control very easily, we're most concerned about one particularly negative effect the drug can have on your bloodstream. The condition is called myelosuppression, meaning your red and white blood cells and your platelets could take a dive.

"So, we will monitor your bloodwork regularly, every Wednesday," Schneider continued.

"You're not particularly high-risk for that; for some strange reason it occurs most often in young women as opposed to young men. We've been using the stuff since 2003, and I can only think of one young man who went profoundly myelosuppressed in that time."

"Do you follow so far?" he asked, searching our faces. Again we nodded, feigning confirmation.

In fact, it was more—dreadfully more—than we could take in. But I knew from our last encounter that Schneider was a phone call away to answer our stray questions and fill in the gaps. Being available to his patients was how Schneider showed he cared.

"Radiation will be administered through high-injection beams," said Schneider, "by a technique called IMRT—Intensity Modulated Radiation Therapy. It's an advanced mode of high-precision radiotherapy that delivers precise radiation directly to the tumor by modulating or controlling the intensity of the radiation beam in multiple small volumes while minimizing damage to the surrounding healthy tissue.

"It's one treatment a day, five days a week in the basement of this building. One treatment lasts about ten to fifteen minutes and is painless. You'll lose your hair in the areas where the beams hit, and you will feel increasingly tired as the treatment progresses. Once you finish treatment, the fatigue goes away. We will do thirty to thirty-two treatments."

It all sounded so simple, like it would come off without a hitch. Like it was no big deal to subject Nate's body to a barrage of toxic chemicals and near-brain-obliterating radiation. Like it wasn't life-altering.

*A brain tumor changes everything* said the poster. How could we have known that "everything" was so far-reaching?

"And afterward . . . another MRI to determine if the treatment's been effective?" I asked. *Dear God, what a dangerous question. Just focus on what's next. It's enough. No need to steer the conversation into the terrifying unknown.*

"Another MRI will be done four to five weeks afterward because we want the whole treatment to have effect. While the radiation damages cells right away, we won't know its effect until the cells try to divide into two and they can't. The time it takes for them to shrink down and die takes about four to five weeks."

"Tell me more about how the surrounding healthy tissue responds to the radiation," I said. The struggle to comprehend the medical vocabulary was staggering. It no longer came in dribbles; rather, it gushed forth like a geyser. Thank God for my recorder.

"The surrounding tissue determines the total dose of radiation we can give," explained Schneider.

"We can safely give the whole brainstem 5,400 centigrays of radiation. At that level, it will not ruin your ability to think, learn, or concentrate," he said, turning to Nate. "Whereas, if you give 6,000 centigrays to the cortex part of the brain, there's about a 5 percent chance of causing significant damage in five years."

"So, you're giving Nate the maximum dose?" I asked. Was he really implying that Nate would receive the maximum dose? And what exactly did he mean by "ruin"? Would we recognize Nate after this treatment? Would he be brain damaged? *Don't panic. Stay focused.*

"Yes, we can administer 5,900 to an area at the back of the brain here," he said, pointing to the base of his neck, "which comes right up against the brainstem—that procedure has been safely done. But this tumor is more in the brainstem, so we've got to be a little more conservative."

Myelosuppression? Centigrays? It was all so technical and utterly mind-boggling.

As if sensing the overwhelmed mood in the room, Schneider turned to Nate. "You're in school now aren't you?"

"Not yet," said Nate. "I'm going back in January—I'm in marketing at the University of Winnipeg."

How far away that dream seemed now, but how necessary to hold on to the future in a shape that seemed familiar to him. Not unlike most patients who passed through these doors, Nate could not begin to understand how life would change once this plan was put in motion.

"Do you have trouble walking?" Schneider asked Nate.

"No," said Nate.

The question was profoundly unsettling. We were at a loss about what to expect from day to day. Questions like this pressed on the precariousness of Nate's condition, though we pushed them aside, needing to survive the present.

"When do you want to start treatment?" Norm asked.

"We'll get the paperwork started today," replied Schneider. "Early next week, probably Monday or Tuesday, we'll conduct the simulation, which just means we'll take more measurements and make a customized plastic mask for your head to keep it in place for the radiation sessions.

"The actual radiation treatments will begin about ten days later," he continued, "because the process is quite involved and needs to be checked by the physics people. It all takes time."

"So, this is the best treatment plan available in North America—in the world?" I asked.

How does one make such an enormous, life-altering decision in the span of a forty-minute meeting? How much medical evidence is enough? Is it even possible to know with certainty that all options have been considered? Where was the panel of global experts? Why on God's green earth should we take Schneider's word on this?

"Let me explain," said Schneider, taking a breath. I had a feeling we were about to get schooled. But not in a way that would make us feel stupid for asking the question, or for questioning his authority. Rather, it would be in a way that would prove his competence in the field and reassure us of the process.

"I've done the research," he said, "and there's no specific information about temozolomide and tectal glioma. There isn't any because it's so uncommon. But we use it all the time for high-grade brain tumors in general. Until the mid-1970s, all medicine could do was perform surgery to remove the tumor. Then, in the later 1970s, they added whole-brain radiation and, soon after, radiation to local parts of the brain.

"The next big advance in treating high-grade brain tumors," he explained, "came out in 2005, some thirty years later with the introduction of temozolomide alongside radiation. This pairing is still the single best treatment to date, but there are probably a hundred trials going on all over the world to determine even more effective targeted therapies. I will say this—it's a hell of an improvement since I started in brain tumors fifteen years ago."

"So, you're saying it's the best treatment option available to us now?" I said.

"Yes, and we're always reviewing it," replied Schneider. "Every Friday at noon, we hold a brain tumor conference here at the hospital that includes doctors, radiologists, and surgeons in the field, and we discuss our cases together. Nate's case will be reviewed on a regular basis."

"Before you leave," Schneider said to Nate, "we need your signature on this form so we can give you blood transfusions if you adversely react to the temozolomide."

And that was it. Nate's scrawl, permanently inked at the bottom of the page, authorized the CancerCare machine to roll forward. There was no turning back now.

How do I describe the feelings following that meeting? Medicine was throwing all its latest discoveries into Nate's body in hopes of slowing the growth of the tumor.

Conspicuously missing from our meeting with Schneider was any whisper of survival rates. We deliberately steered clear of this question, though science would have offered its prediction. Not once did Schneider hint at it.

Had we known about the Kaplan-Meier curve, the metric by which doctors measure the ferocity of a disease compared with the number of patients surviving over time—and that for high-grade brain tumor patients like Nate, the curve drops sharply until only 5 percent of patients are alive at two years—we would have curled into the fetal position in despair.

In the end, we didn't need to hear this statistic; we knew a version of it in our hearts. We were not naïve to the severity of our situation.

It's just that we refused to allow a number to be our inevitability.

# 8

# The Vision

From Christ's suffering body this blood covered the whole earth and descended into hell, releasing those in bondage. Christ's blood ascended into heaven, where (in a mystical sense) Christ is *still* bleeding "praying for us to the father, and is and shall be as long as we need."

—JULIAN OF NORWICH[1]

"OUR HELP IS IN the name of the Lord, the Maker of heaven and earth." Most nights as I lay on my bed, I whispered those words from Psalm 124:8 as part of the night office, a liturgical form of prayer found in the Book of Hours and prayed the world over by Anglican and Catholics.

I began reciting evening prayers six years ago, but during the months of Nate's illness, the power of this deeply embedded refrain took hold of me and became a fierce declaration.

"Your future isn't determined by the contents in a medical folder," I said to Nate. "Your future is determined by the Lord God Almighty, the Maker of heaven and earth. He alone knows the length of your days."

Yes, these words were true, spoken with a measure of conviction that surprised my own ears. How would they be worked out in the coming weeks? I did not know. *Be still my heart. Be assured that God is in the details, even if the details turn out to be unthinkable.*

---

1. Rolf, *Julian of Norwich*, 88.

A mountain of treatment loomed ahead, promising to extract every ounce of physical, emotional, and spiritual strength. In the wake of the meeting, a well-meaning and medically astute relative, well acquainted with the Kaplan-Meier curve and the potentially lethal side effects of Nate's treatment plan, tried to deter us from medical solutions, steering us instead to a Christian community in California renowned for its healing ministry. She had the trip mapped out for us, offering to make the necessary arrangements and meet us there.

But we withered under the possibility. Traveling across the city with Nate seemed dreadfully precarious, let alone traveling by plane across the continent. The conversation unsettled us to the core: we understood that Nate's condition was terminal, that medicine was limited, and that the cancer in Nate's brain was a Goliath only God could strike down.

In the end, it was our conviction that if God chose to heal Nate, he could do so through the way that seemed most open before us—by partnering with these doctors, through this treatment plan. This was the shape of our mercy.

Every day, twenty-seven Canadians are diagnosed with a brain tumor.[2] Some are in the category of high-grade and imminently life-threatening, like Nate's. For these, a decision is required. Some choose to opt out of treatment, hoping for a quality of life that allows them to enjoy the remainder of their days as measured out by medical statistics. Still others in this country may legally choose an assisted dying process.

We chose in favor of the medical plan presented, and spoke of the upcoming treatments as the method of "eradication," a word our friend Willy had received while praying for Nate's healing.

When we gathered around our dinner table that Friday evening, our son-in-law, Jeff, shared something that turned our seriousness into laughter.

Earlier that afternoon, Jeff had bumped into my oldest brother. Reynold was seven years older than I, a distinguished businessman in the city and committed Harley Davidson biker. Although possessing a gentle heart, Reynold was also a fighter, fierce in his defense of family. When Jeff updated him about the meeting with Schneider, Reynold exclaimed, "Sometimes you've got to look the devil in the eye and tell him to F-off."

His words were the antidote to our heaviness that evening. Laughter erupted at our dinner table as we howled over Jeff's shock at his uncle's vocabulary, and affirmed the truth in Reynold's words.

---

2. Brain Tumour Foundation of Canada, "Facts About Brain Tumours," line 1–2.

An expletive aimed at the darkness was somehow adequate to the task of expressing our anger at this disease, at the brokenness that throbs through humanity, at whatever obstructs us from living life as God intends.

THE NEXT DAY WE devised a diversion, a treatment plan of our own. Something that did not involve disease, doctors, or disinfected hallways. The plan involved a certain canine, heaps of cuteness, and a countryside drive.

She was the runt of the litter, mostly black with little patches of white around her nose, small enough to fit into the palm of my hand. According to her breeder, who was a short and feisty woman named Gail, this tiny Miniature Schnauzer with a slight overbite had entered the world along with six brothers and sisters.

Only, she didn't squirm with life at birth. The smallest of the litter, she had been born dead explained Gail. Yet somehow, thanks to the intervention of a determined vet, the stillborn puppy revived.

"She's a miracle pup and a fighter," the affectionate breeder told us. "She may not be as big as the others, but she sure can hold her own when her siblings pick a play fight. She's overcome so much in her little life."

"Outstanding!" I said. "We'll take her."

That Saturday afternoon, my daughters and I traveled forty minutes north of the city on a mission to pick out a puppy. It was a crazy notion, a hasty decision. What we were thinking? Did we have time to pick out a kennel? What about dog food? Did we have the patience to clean up her puddles or fence off her potty space in the backyard? Probably not. Yet, in the face of all the darkness crowding around us, it suddenly made perfect sense.

The arrival of the pup would be a surprise for Nate, who would be attending a Jets game with his dad that Saturday afternoon. Something like joy found its way into our household that evening. Something like mercy found us, disguised as an adorable ball of fur that we named Ruby.

NATE'S TREATMENTS BEGAN TEN days later, on Wednesday, November 30, three days into Advent, the season in the Christian year when the church prepares for Christ's coming.

Yes, the incarnate God in Christ came 2,000 years ago. But Advent gathers past, present, and future into one moment. It's a time of preparation that asks, "How is Christ—the Alpha and Omega—coming to you now?"

Just how Christ would come to us this year remained a mystery. But the idea of living our tragedy in expectation, under the arc of this promise, brought comfort.

And I would need every ounce of daily comfort, especially the first time I picked up Nate's medication.

My voice was shaking when I approached the pharmacy counter. Wasn't this the same neighborhood drugstore that filled the odd prescription of antibiotics for our family, or advised me on which over-the-counter drug was best for a sinus congestion, or a lingering dry cough, or a nasty poison ivy rash?

"I'm picking up the prescription for Nathan Woltmann," I said to the woman behind the computer. She keyed in his name and looked hard at the screen before calling the pharmacist by name, and motioning to him for help.

"The temozolomide?" said the pharmacist, looking up at me from under his reading glasses. "Are you Nathan's mother?" he added.

"I am," I said, nodding quickly, holding out my provincial health card as proof.

I was ushered to a quiet corner of the pharmacy where each bottle was taken out of the paper bag and carefully discussed in detail. There were fifty-milligram tablets and twenty-five-milligram tablets of temozolomide— "Seventy-five milligrams every day for seven days," explained the pharmacist. There was a bottle containing the anti-nausea drug metoclopramide. "One to be taken with the chemotherapy tablets each morning," said the pharmacist.

"Did CancerCare give you handouts to follow?"

I nodded and managed a timid "yes," while my insides lurched. Maybe it was the reality of seeing the stuff for the first time, or maybe I was suddenly feeling overwhelmed by the responsibility to make sure it was all administered correctly, or maybe it was the five-digit figure on the upper right-hand corner of the chemotherapy bottles. Did it really read $5,000? Was it possible that the cost of this prescription was more than my monthly salary?

"Did they advise you of all the side effects, or would you like me to go over these pages with you?"

"No, I've got them at home," I replied, as the pharmacist fastidiously placed each bottle back into the bag and brought them to the cashier.

"Do you have our Air Miles card?" the woman enthused with a wide smile. "You really must get an Air Miles card," she said. "You'll have enough points for a plane ticket in no time."

I just stood there, stupefied. How had my everyday life become so absurd?

TEMOZOLOMIDE CAPLETS, I WOULD later learn, are a derivative of mustard gas, and every bit as toxic as a ninety-minute intravenous infusion. I had carefully organized the pills in a seven-day container according to the binder of instructions from Dr. Schneider's office. Reading through the pages of side effects for the temozolomide brought instant pangs of anxiety. Early onset symptoms included vomiting, headaches, and fatigue. The possible delayed effects of the drug were far more vicious: balance problems, seizures, blood cancer, and sterility.

At 8:00 a.m. Wednesday morning, Nate swallowed his first cocktail of pills. Later that morning, he attended his first radiation appointment in the basement of CancerCare.

THE WAITING ROOM WAS sparse, enough chairs for twenty people or so. There were flatscreen TVs in every corner of the room, a clever decoy to draw attention away from those massive, three-foot-thick lead doors on the one wall that opened like an oversized elevator into the radiation room.

Above the doors was a neon sign that lit up with the words "Radiation On" every time a patient disappeared into the room and was on the receiving end of the beams inside. It was an ominous sight, that light announcing a deadly form of atomic energy doing battle with an even more deadly form of disease.

The radiation technician called Nate's name. He and I made our way to the office, a small, separate room beside the huge double doors. The details of Nate's file filled the computer screens inside the little office, a picture of him wearing his favorite FXR hoodie displayed on the top right of the screen.

"Your name and date of birth?" asked the technician.

"June 27, 1990," said Nate. And with that, he was admitted through the iron curtain. The light flickering "Radiation On" and "Radiation Off" for other patients would soon be flickering for him, like a pair of hazard lights warning everyone within eyeshot about its severity, its toxicity, its opposition to all things human. "Don't come near," it glowered.

That was as far as I was permitted to go. The remainder of the radiation journey Nate would travel alone. The sheer magnitude of those invincible double doors would see to that.

*HEY GOD, ARE YOU there? It's me, Nate.*

*Can you get through those double doors? I sure hope so. No one else can. It's cold in here, and that smell. . . . At least the bed is long enough. Whoa! That is a massive machine up there. It looks like a spaceship. Wait! Do those huge metal plates move? Will they touch me? Dear God, don't let them come crashing down.*

"Hi Nate, my name is Rosie. I need you to look up and stay still. Remember this mask? I'm going to place it over your face now and attach it to the bed in five places with these clips. In just a minute, I'll return to the computer behind that screen and this machine will rotate around you and do its work. Just close your eyes now, try to relax and listen to your music. Country? My favorite."

*God, this mesh mask is suffocating. Is she gone? I can't turn my head. That sounds like a motor. It's starting to move. What's that beeping? Maybe the radiation light is going on. Wait, what's that, a light? Something feels warm. Just close your eyes. Listen to the music. Breath.*

*Whoa. What is that?*

He wasn't trying to imagine anything; he was just trying to survive the experience when the vision came. He saw the foot of a cross, a wooden cross. There was blood trickling down, splattering onto the rocks below.

"It was like looking through a video camera lens," he told us. "At first, the camera zoomed in on the bloody base of the cross, then slowly, ever so slowly, it panned upward to the feet, battered and bruised, and then eventually up . . . up . . . it moved, to reveal a tattered, beaten body."

The picture was disturbing but Nate could not look away. The camera panned the chest area and zoomed in on one arm . . . until it revealed the nail and the blood. The camera followed the red trail onto the wrist where the blood was collecting, ready to drip.

"As the blood dripped," Nate explained, "I followed it down . . . down . . . down, as if in slow motion. Until it finally hit the back of my head."

That's when he saw himself there, under the cross, the blood hitting him precisely where the machine was sending its beam of radiation. Light and warmth. The image merged with his senses, filling him with awe.

To be sure, the cross of Christ was something Nate had heard about since childhood. He had seen pictures, the kind that accompanied Sunday school stories; he had attended Good Friday services where the Passion of Christ was preached.

"But seeing the cross in that radiation room was altogether different," he said. "As though all that anguish, and that broken-open body was just *for me.*"

Every subsequent trip into the radiation room held possibility: "Could this be what is happening in my brainstem? Could that blood be healing me?"

"To become a mystic, is not (for most) to become an ecstatic in some melodramatic style; but rather to enter into a deep encounter with God in a humble, hidden, and entirely mysterious way," says Emily Griffin, author of *Wonderful and Dark Is This Road*. "It is about God's unfailing love. It is about the mystery of the cross. It is about an encounter with the power of God in the middle of things: an encounter that is hidden, inexpressible, ineffable, and real."[3]

There, in a stark radiation chamber designed to administer the most toxic of treatments aimed at healing the human body, Jesus came. Not dressed in resurrection robes, scrubbed clean of human stains. No. He came naked, bruised, and bloodied. Crushed. Broken. There in the mystery of the cross, Jesus came in suffering solidarity: *with* Nate in this place sealed off to all other human contact; *for* Nate in this enterprise aimed at his healing.

An encounter with God in the middle of things: hidden, inexpressible, ineffable, and real.

"Yes," St. John of the Cross would agree. "Do you perceive it—more light, more love, more hope? I, too, beheld Christ crucified, and it changed me.

"Of this I am sure," the sage would say. "The communications from God penetrate the soul, move the will to love and leave their effect within. The soul, even if it wants to, can no more resist their effect than can a window withstand the sunlight shining on it."[4]

*Hold open your hearts to receive this great mystery.*

All this at the beginning of Advent, no less. Thank God for this comfort. Thank God for this mercy.

---

3. Griffin, *Wonderful and Dark Is This Road*, 27.

4. St. John of the Cross, *The Collected Works*, 181–182.

# 9

# Christmas

When our lives are most barren, when possibilities are cruelly limited, and despair takes hold, when we feel most keenly the emptiness of life, it is then that God comes close to us. This is a day for those suffering loss during Advent, lamenting that just as we are suffering and in need to weep, the world force-feeds us merriment and cheer. But we are not without hope, for it is because we are so empty, having used the last scraps of our resources, that God can move in . . . to work in us, and even to play.

—KATHLEEN NORRIS[1]

NATE'S TWELFTH VISIT TO the basement of CancerCare marked the one-third point in his treatment schedule. At the end, the technician in charge, a bubbly woman named Rosie who had been there during Nate's very first appointment, unclamped the mask that firmly fastened Nate's head to the radiation bed.

"So, what are your plans for the rest of the day?" Her question would have been innocuous enough if it had come from a grocery clerk at a checkout line or a Starbucks employee at a drive-through window. But it probably wasn't so trivial coming from someone who had just administered maximum strength, high-intensity radiation beams to another person's brainstem.

1. Norris, "Fourth Monday of Advent," 105.

Rosie would be aware of the debilitating fatigue that accumulates in a body as it fights to repair the damage done to healthy cells after being relentlessly pounded by both radiation and chemotherapy—so debilitating that patients often collapse on a couch for hours afterward.

She would be well acquainted with radiation-induced swelling in the treatment area, a condition called edema, which raises the pressure in the brain, causing headaches, nausea, and, in some cases, seizures.

She would be the first to notice the nasty burn marks where radiation beams had made contact with the skin, causing hair to fall out and skin to break down. There were five such spots on Nate's skull now, perfectly round and bald and slightly raw.

She knew all this.

"I'm going for a skate," announced Nate with an unusual air of confidence.

"Wait! What!?" she asked in disbelief.

"I'm going for a skate," Nate repeated resolutely. "I intend to shoot a puck or two later."

Rosie floated out of the room behind Nate. "This guy's going for a skate," she announced to her colleagues who were equally enamored by the news. They cooed and waved to Nate as if he were a visiting celebrity.

*What's all this happy kerfuffle about?* Perplexed and curious, I waited for Nate to appear in the waiting room.

It was December 15. The last few weeks had not been easy.

Three days into treatment, Nate's nausea had increased, and he had become extremely agitated. I noticed his incessant foot-tapping and fidgeting.

An astute nutritionist at CancerCare noticed the restlessness during one of our meetings.

"Are you on metoclopramide for nausea?" she asked after Nate excused himself from the conversation, pacing the floor. "Because it can cause this level of irritation."

"Yes," I said.

We were promptly escorted down the corridor to the brain tumor clinic. Fortunately, we caught up with Schneider before he left for the weekend. He confirmed that Nate was having a reaction to the anti-nausea drug and prescribed a much more effective and expensive alternative called ondansetron, which suppressed the nausea, enough so Nate could eat foods to help his body.

The nutritionist had advised plenty of protein, more than twice the normal recommended amount in fact. At 120 grams per day, that meant enormous servings of eggs, white meat, and Greek yogurt shakes supplemented with protein powder.

After the agitation incident, body aches and fatigue had caught up with Nate. Weekdays revolved around pill-taking, protein-enriched meals, radiation appointments, short walks and drives, and plenty of naps, preferably while watching TSN in the afternoon. We had purchased a puffy recliner for sleeping and TV-viewing with Ruby, who had cuddled her way into everyone's hearts.

Now he wanted to skate. Shinny hockey, a Canadian pastime and Nate's favorite winter sport, was something he hadn't done since last year—something he wondered if he would ever do again.

With today's resolve came a surge of doubt. Could he hold his balance on a set of blades? Would his double vision interfere with his ability to shoot a puck? Would he survive five minutes of exertion? Was he ready for the heartbreak if the answer to all three questions was "no"?

I listened to my son's doubts and had a few of my own. Where had this sudden burst of energy come from? Would it dissipate like so many other ambitious thoughts in the wake of treatment? And what then? But I said none of this out loud.

By evening, Nate's desire was still alive. We drove past the neighborhood rink. Just a few kids left on the ice.

"I'll skate around for no more than ten minutes," said Nate.

His hands were shaking as he laced up his skates. I parked close by and stayed in full view. My eyes were fixed on the lone figure gingerly taking his first steps onto the rink, hockey stick in hand.

*Dear God, don't let him fall.*

When Nate's skates hit the ice, his adrenaline and muscle memory took over. Within minutes, he was gliding around the rink at full speed, shooting pucks at the net, and smashing rebounds off the boards. There, under the light of the full moon, in the crisp December air, a young man's dreams revived. God, what a sight! What could be more beautiful?

*Wait. Where is his helmet? Why hadn't I insisted? Jesus, protect him. That head is full of radiation—one slip, one knock to the head on that unforgiving ice and his life could be over.*

"Maybe," something whispered. "But maybe it's enough to revel in this moment of glory."

And I did, for the next twenty agonizing, resplendent minutes.

Later that evening, Norm and Kate arrived home from the Jets game. During the warmup, one of the players had sent a puck high over the boards. Despite the wall of netting and all the hands stretching to catch it, the puck landed safely beside Kate's seat like it possessed a secret guidance system. Kate wanted Nate to have it after she heard about his legendary skate.

"Holy mischief," I said.

Then, using a permanent silver marker, I printed the word *hope* on the belly of that puck.

To THIS DAY, I don't know why I violated my personal vow, why I crossed the line on the evening of December 21. But I did. Maybe because I recognized the credibility of the author, maybe because I was looking for some shred of hope, or maybe because the title of the treatise resonated with the life I was living. Maybe something deep inside me just needed to know.

Whatever the reason, and against my better judgement, I clicked on the link that opened up a thesis titled "Who cares for the caregiver? How are the needs of caregivers of primary malignant brain tumour patients met through structured neuro-oncology programs in Canadian Centres?"[2]

The 194-page document was written in 2011 by Orit Reuter, our social worker at CancerCare, as part of her graduate studies program. Orit was assigned to our case from the beginning, when Nate was diagnosed with a benign low-grade brain tumor.

Standing just a little over five-feet tall with shoulder-length, curly brown hair and wire-rimmed glasses, Orit was a small but mighty force. With wizard-like deftness, she cleared the path for any work-related medical leaves, first for Nate when he underwent surgery and then for me after Nate's cancer diagnosis.

She appeared in our clinic room, often unannounced, explained the necessary paperwork and instructed Dr. Schneider where to sign. Without asking for permission, she told us how to proceed. She knew what we were eligible for and how to navigate the employment compensation process. Not many people think about these types of details in a medical crisis. Not many count the financial cost. Orit did.

Upon Orit's recommendation, I applied for compassionate care benefits through my employment insurance plan to take care of Nate through treatment.

"Don't get too worked up about the application," she said. "It sounds a lot more serious than it actually is."

But the description on the application—"paid to people who have to be away from work temporarily to provide care or support to a family member

---

2. Reuter, "Who Cares for the Caregiver," i.

who is gravely ill and who has a significant risk of death within twenty-six weeks"[3]—said otherwise.

Nate's diagnosis and treatment—his life-threatening illness—qualified me for financial assistance. Caregiving was all-consuming and application forms were a nuisance; but checks arriving by mail provided a level of consolation. Orit knew that, too.

Orit was our cheerleader. Her counseling services were available for Nate and our family at no expense. Nate sat with her from time to time after his radiation treatments. She was especially fond of him.

"Come see me when you need a boost," she said.

It was Orit who convinced us that Nate should apply for the Canadian government's income assistance program. She patiently heard our objections. Yes, of course, Norm and I could support Nate financially through this time.

"But he is twenty-one," she said, "and twenty-one-year-olds are young adults who should be drawing an income, which Nate is unable to do right now. Apply for it." Her argument was convincing.

Orit held Nate's dignity and psychological needs with the greatest of care as we made our way through the perilous voyage of the brain tumor world and the uncharted territory of CancerCare. She was a necessary guide.

Now, Orit's thesis was on my screen. What did this trusted companion have to say?

The acronym PMBT, used for patients with primary malignant brain tumors was all over the opening pages—defined, described, disturbing. Was Nate a PMBT patient? This revelation was surprisingly hard to admit. By no means was I on friendly terms with the word cancer—and now PMBT. Surely this wasn't Nate.

My mouth went dry. The tears falling down my cheeks provided a clue. Yes, Nate's tumor was primary, meaning that the mutated cells originated in the brain and, yes, it was now malignant, the MRI showed evidence of growth.

*Stop reading. Stay with your present knowledge. Don't get ahead of yourself. Shut the laptop.*

I kept reading.

Until now, we had successfully avoided stepping on the conversational landmines, such as statistics, probabilities, lifespan. Schneider didn't offer. We didn't ask. Most people steered clear of the question.

It took just a few sentences to tell the story we were hell-bent on avoiding. A few sentences distilled the cruel facts into a small cluster of words.

3. Government of Canada, "End-of-life Care," lines 1–3.

"The diagnosis and grade determines the treatment and prognosis with low-grade survival being approximately four and a half years and high-grade, twelve months (with treatment) . . . Despite technological advances in medicine, like targeted radiation techniques and chemotherapy, the prognosis for PMBT remains lethal."[4]

I closed the computer screen, shutting out the facts.

The word *lethal* echoed in my brain and body. Lethal. It cut through my bone and marrow and sliced open my heart. Lethal. Maybe Orit was wrong. She wasn't a doctor.

Norm was in the next room watching TV, completely oblivious. Nate was in the basement catching up on his sports shows. I sat alone in the dim light of the living room on the winter solstice.

*But wait. Wasn't it just last week that Nate had visited Orit in her office?*

"This feels like a death sentence," he said then.

"It doesn't have to be," she said. "You're young, your body is strong."

Tomorrow, daylight would be extended by one minute, and by another minute every day until June 21, the summer solstice, the longest day of the year, just a few days before Nate's birthday. His twenty-second birthday. Exactly six months from today.

Where would we be then? And after that? And next Christmas?

*God Almighty, stop thinking!*


SOMETIME DURING THE MONTH of December, I managed to put up our tree. Ours was the boxed kind and at least a decade old. I hadn't wanted to pull it out of its home in the garage rafters. It was a symbol of joy and merriment— and I felt neither. There were just too many happy memories in that box and unleashing them would be unbearable.

In the end, a good friend reminded me to do it for the sake of my kids. It was true, the girls expressed excitement about the season despite the lingering sadness in our home.

We hauled up the boxes of decorations from the basement, placing the golden baubles on the tree and adding a new ornament in the shape of a black Miniature Schnauzer with the words "Ruby's First Christmas" hand-printed on the bottom. After scouring hardware stores and online sites, we even managed to buy strings of vintage-looking colored lights to replace the twinkling white ones. Nate's idea.

On December 23, I visited my friend Jeannette. She and her husband had just returned from fighting the holiday crowds at Costco. Crates of goodies crowded the counter space on her island.

4. Reuter, "Who Cares for the Caregiver," 6–9.

"Come to the living room," she said when she saw my face.

I told her about the thesis and the word "lethal." I sobbed in her living room, among the perfectly arranged Christmas candles and assortment of gifts spilling out from under the pine tree. Jeannette listened and cried. I can't remember what she said, but I do remember sharing the tissue box she put between us.

"Have you told Norm?" she asked.

"Yes, last night," I said.

Norm and I had made dinner reservations to celebrate his last day of work before the holidays. On the drive, I confessed the whole of it.

Both of us had agreed not to look on the internet. Period. My actions had violated our agreement. I knew that full well. I expected my husband to be annoyed, maybe even angry. I would have been. Instead, he listened to all the ugly details. There in the cab of the truck, he breathed deeply and spoke gently into my stormy sea of words.

"We will live whatever time is left with Nate to the full," he said.

My heart welled up with love for my husband. This man who was doing his best to provide for us on three days a week at the office. This man who ended our tearful evening conversations with the words, "Well done." This man who shared the care for our son on his days off, engaging in whatever distraction proved helpful. This man.

I said goodbye to Jeannette, feeling better that someone shared our plight. This is the miracle of friendship, that she was willing to bear it with me.

"Blessed are the available," became a gospel beatitude that day. Blessed are those who stop in the middle of all things bustling and brimming with merriment and cheer, who choose an hour of raw grief over a kitchen full of Christmas preparations. Blessed are those who choose to share sorrow.

Maybe that's the whole point Jesus was trying to make with his friends Mary and Martha. Mary, full-hearted, all ears, attentive to the God-man in her living room on death watch. Martha, distracted by all those mouths to feed. Jesus said only one thing was needed and Mary chose the better.

But the better often comes at an enormous emotional cost. Blessed are the available.


THOUGHTS, LIKE WISPS OF vapor, never rest. And when we sleep, thousands of busy neurons chase them down on well-worn pathways through the brain, problem solving, imagining, stirring up feelings of dread.

Christmas Eve dawned. In my waking, I could feel my body clutched by fear, sounding its primordial response to threat, every muscle on high alert. *Lethal.* That word emerged from my early-morning mist of thoughts; it inhabited my psyche and paraded through my mind with its cohorts: *twelve months, with treatment.*

What if this is his last Christmas? Should we tell the girls? Tears fell. I rolled over to touch Norm, to place myself against him, and was quite sure he was wrestling down the same early morning demons. He took my hand and we held each other tight, a wordless knowing.

We couldn't discuss it then. I could hear Nate's steady breathing coming from the floor beside Norm.

We had purchased a five-inch foam mattress when Nate began treatment. Then, there was no telling how the treatments would affect him, the pages of possibilities reading like something out of a torture manual from a war chamber: hair loss, skin burns, swelling in the brain, weakness in an arm or leg, speech problems, balance problems, muffled hearing.

The best of human logic didn't stand a chance against the anxiety that list produced, especially for Nate. It was *his* body and *his* brain being taken to the very brink of its defenses; would it hold?

Nights felt safer together. Often, in the deep darkness, when Nate would toss and turn, Norm would stretch out his hand and place it firmly on Nate's back or shoulder. His physical presence was an antidote to Nate's fearful restlessness. We all need a steady hand to hold us through the terror; someone to watch over us in our fitful sleep. Norm was a tireless watchman.

I was loath to get out of bed, to touch my feet to the floor in the daily act of rising. Instead, I wanted to lie there with my husband and gaze at our son, daring time to slow down.

I had read tales of how holidays highlighted pain for people. Other people, that is. Just as these people suffer and need to weep, the world force-feeds merriment. I had heard such things, even participated in a "Blue Christmas" service. But my best imagining was an impoverished substitute for the experience of the thing itself. *So, this is what a Blue Christmas feels like.*

Any other year, I would have jumped out of bed with a list of last-minute errands: fresh cold cuts from the meat market, fresh buns from the corner bakery, a few more appetizers to round out the evening meal (as if more were needed—the freezer was bursting with enough options for a week). Always, there were a few last-minute gifts to wrap: a pair of socks, a set of earrings, a coffee mug—impulsive purchases to round out the burgeoning collection under the tree (as if more were needed—the tree was bursting with enough treasures).

Any other year, we would have attended the Christmas Eve service at our downtown church in the late afternoon and enjoyed a not-so-light meal afterwards—good food arranged in bowls and platters around the soft light of votive candles.

From the time our kids were small, this meal was the necessary ritual that preceded our much-anticipated gift exchange. The chatter around the table would have been charged with excitement and a kindly parental reminder *not to hurry*.

But this was not just any other year. A Christmas Eve service was out of the question. We avoided public places because they threatened Nate's immune system and our sanity. Our skin was worn so thin by grief, one careless comment by the most well-intentioned and we might bleed out in all directions.

There were still gifts to be opened under the tree, a modest amount. We picked names, even Norm and I, and capped the purchase at fifty dollars each. We had neither the energy nor the means to be lavish.

In the end, we prepared a simple meal and took pleasure in the candlelight and the extravagance of one another's presence.

There was another annual ritual, too—an unusual one, not always popular with our children over the years. But this Christmas, light shone through it and dispelled the darkness, if only for a few sacred minutes. I can still feel its power.

The tradition began ten years ago in an effort to make our time together more meaningful and personal. After the meal, and before the floor was littered with paper, bows and boxes, we would exchange a gift of words, a blessing. When we started, all three kids were in elementary school.

The annual practice involved writing a sentence or two of genuine appreciation and encouragement for each family member on a yellow sticky note. Each family member received an identical Christmas card where the notes were placed and—we hoped—their power planted.

Yes, there was some resistance when we had introduced the idea to our preteens. Eye-rolling and grumbling ensued. But Norm and I persisted.

We focused on one person at a time, usually in the order of youngest to oldest. In the early days, the kids wrote things like, "I think you're good at soccer and I like being your sister," or "Thanks for taking me to the mall last week, Dad, I enjoyed it."

Of course, Norm and I would prepare more elaborate and intimate notes for each family member, highlighting growth in character and expressing our love and pride with carefully chosen words like, "Laura, you have a compassionate nature that attracts the seniors at your workplace. This is a gift. Cherish it. We love you and can't wait to see how your gifts will unfold as you grow." Or, "You have an adventurous spirit, Kate, and a keen desire to learn—may you sense God's direction as you find ways to nurture your inner explorer."

Such words were received with shy smiles, even gratitude. The practice had opened our hearts to one another in a way that utterly subverted the giving and receiving of the material gifts under the tree.

Blessings have a way of doing this.

This year, I had bought a playful set of cards to hold the notes. Pictured on the front were twelve puppies dressed in jackets, toques, and scarves, their shaggy little profiles resembling our Miniature Schnauzer. It was Ruby's first Christmas, after all. At the very least, the cards would evoke smiles.

Writing the blessings to go inside was another matter. We all agonized over what to say, our small and insignificant ritual now a portal where true thoughts and feelings could take shape, maybe one last time.

A playful card with puppies would hold our love in sentences that could be read and reread now and in years to come. It took all afternoon and all our courage to write a few words. And far more to read them aloud.

WE FORM A CIRCLE in the glow of the vintage-colored tree lights, shuffling our sticky notes like small decks of cards, suddenly awkward. Who should be first to receive? We agree to a reversal this time. Instead of youngest to oldest, we will begin with Laura and Jeff, then Kate, and finally Nate. Parents will be last.

When it is Nate's turn to receive, Laura bravely begins. She focuses on reading her words, although I notice her eyes carry a look of sadness. They seem strained underneath their usual blue, far too full of grief for a twenty-five-year-old.

"This year has not been easy for you," Laura reads. "I marvel at the growth in your relationship with Jesus and your faith in him. You encourage me. I am so proud of you. You haven't just encouraged people around you, you have encouraged people you haven't even met! I love you very much and I'm so proud to be your sister."

Jeff is three years into the ritual and always brings wit and humor. But this time his blessing is serious and measured, "You have been both a great inspiration and example to me. I am amazed at your faith and your openness to share that faith with others. I trust God that 2012 will bring healing to your body and I look forward to celebrating that with you."

Next comes Kate. She, who exudes whimsy and bubbles over with laughter, now says softly, "Nate, you are the most amazing brother ever. I don't know how I got so lucky. Your character makes you stand out in a crowd. God is always present in you and it is so amazing to see the difference you're making in so many lives. I love you so much."

After the three speak their blessings, they bring their notes to where Nate is sitting in the circle, hugging him tight and long.

Norm clears his throat and steadies his voice before reciting the words on his sticky note.

"Nate, I am so proud of you and love you very much. You continue to live out God's love with a fire that burns inside you. You are such a blessing to me. You are so courageous and strong and God's presence is all over you. I love to be with you as we drive or just sit together—you give me life. God has blessed us with you, and together we look forward to watching God use you powerfully in his kingdom. I love you very much and wouldn't leave my wingman."

"Wingman"—that term of endearment still brings me to tears. "Dad, my wingman," Nate says, as he chokes out his blessing, "you strengthen me and hold my hand through the toughest times. You are courageous and brave and you comfort me every day. You show me what it is to be a man of God. You are a gift."

They hug and cry.

It's my turn. I can barely speak over the emotion that sits in my throat like a rock. The love that fills the room is palpable, uncontainable by human standards.

What are the words of the Nicene creed? *God from God, Light from Light, true God from true God . . . he came down from heaven.*

Incarnation. God with us, made flesh. Or, in the words of theologian Eugene Peterson, God making himself at home in the neighborhood. God arriving into darkness, hostility and bondage, into a manger of borrowed space and real time, into human ruin. Becoming limited.

He still comes down. I see him sitting among us, there in our blessing exchange. He is crying our tears and sharing our smiles, fully present to our joy and grief.

*God from God, Light from Light, true God from true God.*

In the most intimate of human circles, a family, a people bound together by an eternal love, it is possible for sorrow to shine.

Alexander Schmemann describes it well:

> Little by little, we begin to understand, or rather to feel, that this sadness is indeed "bright," that a mysterious transformation is about to take place in us. It is as if we were reaching a place to which the noises and the fuss of life, of the street, of all that which usually fills our days and even nights, have no access, a

place where they have no power. . . . It is not the noisy and the superficial happiness which comes and goes twenty times a day and is so fragile and fugitive; it is a deep happiness which comes . . . from our soul having, in the words of Dostoevsky, touched "another world." And that which it has touched is made up of light and peace and joy, of inexpressible trust.[5]

I begin my blessing, looking directly at Nate.

"You are a mother's delight," I say.

"But far more than that, you are a delight to your heavenly father. Challenged by the greatest struggle in life, your spirit is responding with a rugged and fierce beauty that is rare for one so young.

"Your life is a light that God has placed on a lampstand; his glory shines through you, son. I love you.

"Forever."

---

5. Schmemann, *Great Lent*, 32–33.

# 10

# The Slaughter

When Herod saw that he had been tricked by the wise men, he was infuriated
and he sent and killed all the children in and around Bethlehem who were two
years old or under, according to the time that he had learned from the wise
men. Then was fulfilled what had been spoken through the prophet Jeremiah:
A voice was heard in Ramah, wailing and loud lamentation, Rachel weeping
for her children; she refused to be consoled, because they are no more.

—MATTHEW 2:16–18 (NRSV)

HAD SHE KNOWN THE horror that would visit her forgotten little town that
night, she would have hidden herself and the boy in the hills. But there was
no warning: no star, no dream, no whisper of dread in the moonlit sky.

Sara settled in the little town of Bethlehem like generations of her
kinfolk. Barely seventeen, she was the mother of a toddler named Benjamin
and married to her childhood sweetheart, Jacob.

Now she was six months pregnant, with Benjamin hanging on her
skirt wherever she went in the village. He was her heart's delight: bouncy
loose curls and ebony eyes that stared back at her, all pooled in innocence
and curiosity.

Hers was a charmed life, of this she was sure. Yahweh's favor rested
on Bethlehem and its destiny. A baby born at the same time as Benjamin
was rumored to be the Messiah, the one who would save her people from

the tyranny of the Roman Empire and the wicked heart of its appointed king, Herod.

How odd that this tiny Messiah was Benjamin's playmate. How odd that Yahweh's help was wrapped in small skin. But there was no mistaking his arrival: angel choirs had appeared to the town's shepherds, like Eli, her neighbor. His description still gave her goosebumps.

"Like the sky was on fire with light and sound in holy harmonies," he said, "ushering us into the very folds of heaven, our bodies alive to its vibrations."

And more recently, foreigners, draped in robes befitting royalty, had come in search of the famous little family, to see the God-child for themselves. They were students of the night sky with its shifting constellations, including a star that insisted they follow it to Bethlehem. It was said that they had brought gold and exotic oils for the baby. How lucky she was to live at this time in history.

The night was still and calm and the community blissfully sleeping when the earth began to tremor. It was easy to mistake the sound of a hundred hooves for thunder.

Shouting soldiers shattered the night silence.

"Come out of your houses, you filthy dogs!" they bellowed. "Show yourselves to the army of Herod!"

The village menfolk, dazed and dressed in nightshirts were no match for the brass-plated warriors brandishing swords.

Screams, thick and guttural reached Sara's ears before the full assault arrived at her doorstep.

"Hide yourself and the child!" shouted Jacob.

She was huddled in the furthest corner of their home, stifling Benjamin's sobs while Jacob feverishly moved what little furniture they owned in front of the bolted door.

Even so, they came: their bodies crashing through the opening, swords flashing in the moonlight, eyes glistening moist with hate.

"Where are they?" one roared.

Jacob's body slumped to the floor, as he died resisting their force.

And how she wished she, too, had died when the sounds of Benjamin's sobs ceased and his body lay limp in her arms, his lifeblood pooling on the floor like that of a little lamb.

She blacked out then, the baby inside her belly wildly kicking its protests.

There was nothing silent or holy about that night in Bethlehem, nothing calm or bright. On that night, precious infant boys two and under, tender and mild, were slaughtered by the hateful sword of Herod.

"Sleep in heavenly peace," we sing at the cradle of the Christ. But on that night, the heavenly peace of Bethlehem was pierced through by a sword.

It's there, the grizzly tale of human horror, among the sights and sounds of the Christmas story—the longer story that spans the twelve-day celebration in the Christian calendar. While we're still gazing at the nativity, smelling the fresh hay that nestles the Christ Child, listening to the harmonies of angel choirs and glimpsing the glowing faces of two parents under the luminous star of wonder, a disturbing story of evil is in the making.

Herod, the leader of the Jewish people under the authority of Rome hears news from the Magi that a king has been born in the land, *his* land. Such a threat to his power must be eradicated, so he orders his army to kill all male children two and under in and around Bethlehem. Warned by an angel in a dream, Joseph narrowly escapes to Egypt with Mary and the Christ Child. No such warning comes for the others.

Throughout Christian history, it has been named the Slaughter of the Holy Innocents. It is a jarring narrative that tears at the very fibers of salvation; it's the embodiment of all that is wrong and crooked in the world. Yet, it is a story that's been told and retold from the very earliest centuries of the church on the first Sunday after Christmas, even today.

It is a day to remember those first small martyrs. It is a day to hear—to really hear—the cries of the broken-hearted mothers of Bethlehem as they come to us through the bitter tears of Rachel.

"Bend your ear and listen," St. Matthew beckons. "Listen to Rachel, the ancient mother, long dead, buried near that little town, weeping, wailing, refusing to be comforted in the wake of the violence. Can you hear her?"

How often had I skipped over this part of the Christmas story. Yet, on the last Sunday of December, in 2011, it offered a pathway for my grief.

If the incarnation, God with us, could be proclaimed in the presence of "Rachel weeping for her children," then this gospel had room for me, too, not only beside the manger, but also inside the tears of this motherhood. Their hearts, like mine, were pierced and sorely wounded. Yes, Mary would join this company of women soon enough. A sword would pierce the side of her son, too, before his young-adult form lay lifeless in her arms at the foot of the cross.

The Pieta. No wonder this image, famously envisioned by Michelangelo, has often served as the subject for artists and sculptors. No wonder the Pieta holds the gaze of mothers the world over. It is the universal shape of maternal compassion, the posture we were born to imitate—a deep and divine impulse that desires to bear all things.

Yet who wants to look upon scenes of suffering in a season swooning with sparkle, amidst a society that insistently says: "Be of good cheer!" But look we must, says the Gospel writer, at the manger, at the broken-hearted mothers of Bethlehem bent over their baby boys and, further still, to the broken-hearted Mary bent over the broken body of her grown son.

And what if we could see in the timeless Pieta another image? Could we see God, in the crucified Christ, bent over each mother, cradling her, holding her tight, crying her tears, bearing her sorrow?

For this is the shape of incarnation, the great gospel reversal, the paradox of faith: It is God in the crucified Christ who bends over *our* pierced and broken hearts, bearing us up with a fierce tenderness, crying our tears, sharing our sorrows, taking us into herself with all the maternal energy that birthed creation.

"The blessed wounds of our Savior are open and rejoice to heal us," says Julian of Norwich. "The sweet, gracious hands of our mother are ready and diligent about us."[1]

IN THE EARLY HOURS of December 27, Nate had a dream, more like a nightmare. The dream was so vivid, so disturbing, so violent that Nate was unable to speak about it for days. It was a slaughter and he was a willing participant . . . maybe even a murderer.

And when, at last, he worked up the courage to tell me about it on one of our afternoon drives, a chill ran up and down my spine. I understood why it haunted him.

"You've been unusually quiet these last two days, Nate," I began cautiously after twenty minutes of silence on the all-too-familiar roadway that snaked along the river. He was staring vacantly out the passenger window, wiping away stray tears with the back of his hand.

"What's going on Nate, what's wrong?" I asked. "Does it have anything to do with Christmas being over? Do you feel a kind of emotional letdown?"

"I had a dream," he blurted, "and part of it still spooks me."

I sat up a little straighter in my seat. Dreams can be powerful avenues of revelation, a way to hear from God without the vigilance of our familiar and reasoned neural pathways. In our half-sleep state, that state of REM when our prefrontal cortex works overtime to process our experiences and our usual defenses can't get in the way, we are vulnerable to different ways of knowing.

1. Rolf, *Julian of Norwich*, 147.

Not all dreams demand our attention, but some possess a quality too strong to ignore. I was all ears now.

"Oh," I said, trying to sound unfazed, relieved for this small opening, "Do you want to talk about it?"

"Yeah—I think so," he said in a hushed tone.

"It was all so innocent and comforting at first," Nate's words came slowly, almost apologetically, his eyes still fixed on the scenery whizzing past his window. "The dream, I mean."

"Go on," I said.

"I was in a cabin, warming myself by the fire. Another man stood beside me. I didn't know him, but I knew immediately he was a friend. It was so warm and peaceful, I could have stayed there forever.

"But then the man spoke saying, 'It's time.' I was confused. 'Time for what?' I asked.

"'It's time for the ambush,' said the man. 'Here, take this sword. Follow me.'"

Nate stopped in the telling and looked directly at me for the first time. "Weird, right?" he said emphatically. "The guy used the word *ambush*. I mean, who even uses that language? I barely know what it means. And a sword? Where did that come from? Maybe a gun would have made more sense, but a sword? In what world?"

"What happened next?" I coaxed, not wanting to stray too far from the story.

"I was dazed, in a kind of stupor. But I followed him anyway, into the rolling hills surrounding the cabin. It didn't occur to me to resist. He was a bigger guy, really fit, like a Navy Seal-type, a guy you wouldn't want to mess with," Nate said, his voice registering a hint of excitement, his hands outlining the enormity of the man's shape.

"He led me into a patch of tall grass at the crest of a hill and told me to get down. Told me to cover myself with grass. 'Don't move,' he said. We just lay there, completely still, camouflaged for what seemed like hours. That's when I heard it."

Nate paused again to look out the window, seemingly lost in the memory.

"Heard what?" I asked, "What did you hear?"

"Footsteps." Nate said, coming out of his reverie. "Hundreds of footsteps against the earth. They were advancing toward us on the other side of the hill. And they were chanting something chilling in a language I didn't understand. It sounded like a war cry. I remember thinking: *What's going on? Why do I have a sword? Who's trying to kill me?* My heart was beating so wildly in my chest, I thought I would die."

Nate paused for a breath and I became aware that I was holding mine. "And then?" I asked in a half whisper.

"Through a small opening in the grass, I could see them emerge," Nate said. "Dark figures, black from top to bottom, not human in shape. Thousands of them came, marching, and chanting, forming a shadowy field at the base of the hill. All of a sudden, the man threw off his grass covering and said, 'Let's go! It's time to attack, follow me!'

"Before I knew it, the man crested the hill and plunged toward the unwary figures, driving his sword through the center of one. I was dazzled by his skill, his precise movements. I could tell he was a trained fighter. And suddenly, I was doing the same, wielding and thrusting my sword into the backs of the unsuspecting enemy. Fluids gushed and our swords glistened.

"I can't remember how long we fought, side by side, gutting the black beings one by one. But I do remember waking up feeling sweaty and stunned. All of them were dead, their bodies littering the open field.

"I know how bad this sounds," Nate said, casting a glance in my direction, "but the truth is, Mom, I thoroughly enjoyed killing those creatures! I reveled in seeing every last one of them die."

His voice trailed off into silence as he slumped in his seat. Was it relief or sadness, or was it the lingering voices of shame and guilt causing him to curl inward?

"That must have been so traumatic," I said into the silence that followed.

I tried to imagine my son on a killing spree of grotesque proportions, but all I could see were images of another kind, a slideshow of stills on fast forward.

Nate at three, not retaliating when his playmate preferred to pinch and bite.

Nate at six, weeping over the loss of his pet hamster, broken-hearted that the little creature, who loved nothing better than to play hide-and-seek in Nate's shirt, had suffered a seizure.

Nate at twelve, with over-sized teeth and a freckled nose, wearing a special vest that identified him as a conflict manager on his school playground, peacemaking and protecting.

Nate at eighteen carrying the casket of his beloved Oma, tenderly laying her to rest at the gravesite.

It's not that Nate couldn't fight, but he was born with an innate sensitivity toward all living things. I understood all too well why this dream troubled him so.

"It was traumatic," Nate agreed. "I was so ashamed. My conscience was screaming at me, 'How could you?' and I was filled with guilt. I don't know how long I stood in front of the bathroom mirror, madly splashing water on my face, trying to purge the dream from my mind. I prayed hard: 'God, I'm so disturbed. How could I enjoy killing those creatures?'"

Silence.

"And then a question came from somewhere inside," he mused, "in a voice that wasn't condemning or harsh or judgmental. 'Nate,' the gentle voice said, 'What were they chanting?' I thought for a minute and then I remembered."

"Remembered what?" I asked earnestly. "What were they chanting?" By this time, I was pinned to my seat and having trouble keeping an even speed on the highway. Thank goodness no one was following us. For once, I was grateful to drive well below the speed limit.

"It was *cancer!*" Nate said, spitting out the word with disdain. "The man told me they were chanting the word *cancer!*"

I let out a gasp and gripped the steering wheel with both hands.

"Cancer," I said breathlessly, and glanced at him in amazement.

His eyes were twinkling now as he unraveled the rest of the story. He told me how, later that same day, the dream narrative began to change. The strangeness of the scene settled on him and got him thinking. The whole thing was beyond his experience: the sword, the ambush, the army in black chanting *cancer*, the warrior guide. He had no context for such things. But it was as if God were speaking to him, "You're in a battle for your life. We have to fight, we have to eliminate the enemy. The stakes are high; the measures are extreme."

It was then, Nate said, that something shifted in his soul and courage began to rise. The dream became a metaphor, the man became a holy messenger.

And fear . . . turned to hope.


We were jolted awake when the phone rang in the early morning of January 5.

The new year had come and gone quietly for our family. Other years, we had gone to Warren and Sandy's cottage with our brood of eight grown children, passing the time with rousing card games and enormous amounts of festive foods.

Not so this year. I had packed up the tree and boxed up the ornaments earlier in the week with a sense of urgency and relief, returning them to the corner of the house where they would stay until next Christmas. Next year . . . what would 2012 bring? The thought was surfacing with annoying persistence. *Stay focused. The finish line for chemotherapy and radiation is in sight now.*

"Hi Jan, it's Kelly from CancerCare," said the voice on the other end of the phone.

"Has Nate taken his temozolomide this morning?"

"No, he's still sleeping," I said, feeling a stab of panic in my chest. "Why?"

"Don't let him take it," Kelly said. "His bloodwork from yesterday came back—he needs to stop chemotherapy immediately!"

"What! Why?" I asked.

"Nate's platelet count is dangerously low," said Kelly, "and his life is at risk if he continues."

Dr. Schneider had warned us about this deadly side effect when we had first met to discuss the treatment plan. The condition was called myelosuppression, and it occurred most often in young women. Schneider recalled only one young man who had reacted negatively to the drug since its inception in 2003.

Now, here we were. The improbable had happened, twelve days away from the finish line, on day thirty-six of a forty-eight-day chemotherapy regimen.

The news was shocking and completely unexpected—a sharp turn in an already precarious journey. For those acquainted with the rhythms of chemotherapy, any interruption to the plan feels like utter defeat, like all of the hell unleashed in a person's body by unrelenting chemicals has been for naught.

Nate's particular treatment plan hinged on the efficacy of chemotherapy *and* radiation. To stop the one was nothing short of cruel.

"I can't believe it," said Nate through tears. "My biggest fear has come true! How can I be the exception to the rule? What's wrong with my body?"

Norm took Nate to his radiation appointment in the basement of CancerCare later that morning while I sought answers at the brain tumor clinic upstairs.

Kelly met me in the waiting room. I was a tangle of tears and questions.

"At this point, we don't know how this will affect the tumor or its advancement," said Kelly. "A platelet crash after five weeks is better than a platelet crash after week one."

Yes, her words were true but of no consolation.

"In the meantime, Nate will finish his course of radiation as planned," said Kelly.

It took half a day to feel a shift in my spirit, to turn again to the truth, to the gentle voice within, reminding me that God Almighty, not Schneider, not the team at CancerCare, was in charge of Nate's treatment plan.

But Nate would have none of it. His heart was decimated. Could God be trusted, he wondered, or was Nate a pawn in some cruel, cosmic storyline?

We met with Dr. Schneider the following week.

"Some say the body responds this way because the chemotherapy has done its job," he said in a philosophical tone, as he leaned against his desk and thrust his hands into the pockets of his white coat. That was all. He looked from Nate to me, and went silent.

Somehow all our desperate questions dissolved into that small opening of hope. After all, this was the genius of Dr. Schneider, his signature of mercy. Not once in our relationship did he say more than was necessary. Not once did he give us any reason to give up.

Maybe, just maybe, in the land of gray matter and neurons, just beyond our perception, was a field full of dead glial cells, ambushed by a secret assault.

The body held the mystery; the dream made us wonder. We wouldn't know for sure for some time. Mercy hinted that we hang on.

# 11

## Liminal

It takes time to get used to this dark, empty, disconnected space. Dark for any lack of waymarks, any maps, any light at the end of the tunnel. Empty of all the meanings that previously guided our life. Empty it feels, even, of meaning itself, for what meaning can there be in this helpless hanging, this waiting room for something that may not even be real or possible. Disconnected from the links that once held us together, bereft of the old relationships, cut off from the old communions and traditions. This is the waiting room, but it feels like a tomb.

—MARGARET SILF[1]

JANUARY 17 DAWNS. THE daytime high is supposed to be a chilling minus thirty degrees Celsius, with sun. While the weather for the first month of 2012 is setting records, so are we. Today is Nate's last radiation appointment, his thirtieth round. Also chilling. When we began our crazy treatment journey on November 30, this day seemed distant, a universe away.

But now we are immersed—for better or worse—in all the ups and downs of this foreign world. I listen for the technician to call Nate's name and look at those seated in the basement waiting room of CancerCare. There are mostly seniors today, clutching tissues and wordlessly waiting with spouses or partners.

---

1. Silf, *Born to Fly*, 113.

Last week, a young boy, maybe ten or so, sat in these chairs with his father. When they called the boy's name, both father and son presented to the technician. The scene was heartbreaking. A brain tumor patient? I would never know, but a cancer patient to be sure.

We are still waiting for Nate's appointment when we're startled by a commotion in the hallway. What's going on? Then we see her, a woman on a stretcher flanked by attendants. They are excitedly talking with each other about how to maneuver the awkward bed and intravenous pole in the narrow hallway. The woman lies quiet and still amidst the clamor. She has come from the hospital for her daily dose of healing.

Nate looks away. His face falls. Scenes like this give claws to the injustice in the room, in the building. Suffering is everywhere. It is on the faces of old and young. The flatscreen TVs in every corner mindlessly flash their cooking shows and celebrity interviews, doing their best to tempt our gaze, distract from our pain. In the end, they fail. Suffering is the unruly beast that holds us hostage.

"Nathan," calls the technician.

"Name and birthdate?" she asks when he appears.

"June 27, 1990," Nate replies.

She smiles and elbows him playfully.

"Come with me," she says. "This is your final visit."

She ushers Nate behind the iron curtain, five feet thick.

Then, I hear it. Music. Loud enough to draw the attention of everyone around me. I quickly recognize the tune and those words. They're from Nate's playlist.

Now it's my turn to smile.

The radiation techs recognize the significance of this moment for Nate, enough to upset the silence of the waiting room, enough to let some song about tattoos and small towns cut through this otherwise solemn space. Smiles unite us. Clearly, the technician has cranked the volume.

Within several minutes, Norm and I exchange knowing glances. So much passes through our eyes. The light above the iron door glows red with the words "Radiation On," announcing the fifth and final time radioactive beams will penetrate Nate's brainstem today.

"It is finished," I whisper.

Norm nods.

Nate emerges from behind the curtain looking triumphant.

"Take good care," says one technician.

"Heal up," says another.

Along with his CD of favorite tunes, Nate is carrying a transparent blue garbage bag with a parting gift—the mesh mask, his helmet of salvation.

I don't know if I should recoil or rejoice at the sight of it. I tell myself that, later, I will carefully examine the mask and take note of the markings, the five "X"s crafted with precision to provide an opening for healing. I never do. Some things are just too hard.

At home, Laura and Kate have prepared a finish-line party, complete with streamers crisscrossing the front entrance. Nate does a full-body lean into the streamers, his hands flailing, his face beaming to the soundtrack of *Chariots of Fire.*

"Hugs all around," says Laura.

"You did it!" screams Kate.

They dance in the afternoon shadows.

THIRTY ROUNDS OF BODILY assault in a radiation chamber; thirty-six doses of maximum-strength chemotherapy. "It won't ruin his ability to think," I hear Schneider say. Even now I pale at the thought. I look at him this morning, still walking and talking as Nate.

But he is altered in ways unseen to all but us. Gone is the energy to skate, to walk, to move about. Eating takes effort. Even after the final treatment, the radiation keeps working, accumulating. His brainstem is full of its rays and swollen beyond recognition.

The distance between dancing and despair is about twelve hours. That's the time it takes for a new reality to surface in the strange land of cancer, before a new terror takes hold.

Until now, the goal has been to survive treatment, to mark success in the form of a black "X" on the calendar at the end of each day. To rip off a countdown sticky on the dining room wall. Until now, the patient has been tethered to shape and purpose via his radiation schedule. When the schedule disappears, the patient and his caregivers experience a freefall, a plunge into the void.

"What does it say?" asks Nate when a letter arrives in the mailbox a few days later.

I open it reluctantly and feel a familiar gnawing in my gut.

"February 17," I say.

"An MRI before four weeks is useless," I hear Schneider say. "The picture would be a blur of indistinguishable tissue."

Now, here it is in black and white—exactly one month to the day until the MRI. And after that? More waiting. Another seven days to finally hear the results from Dr. Schneider within the walls of the brain tumor clinic. Almost forty days of waiting.

And for what? At best, the treatments will have paralyzed the growth of the tumor, allowing Nate more time, likely measured in months, maybe a year. At worst, the treatments will have had no impact and the aggressive tumor will be advancing. I struggle hard to hold this medical opinion alongside the hope of a third way.

A miracle.

Almost forty days—the time between the end of treatment and the knowing, a wilderness, a desert, a Lent.

A few weeks from now, Christians around the globe will walk out of churches into the night, mortality etched with ash on their foreheads. Ash Wednesday will signal the beginning of Lent, a forty-day period of fasting and reflection before Easter. Our Lenten period began the third week of January, as we walked into our night, mortality etched with the ash of suffering on our hearts.

There is a name for this kind of waiting, a name strange to our ears, a name deep enough to hold questions of life and death. That name is *liminal*.

The word liminal is from *limen*, Latin for *threshold*,[2] a place between places, a thin place, where the old no longer fits and the new is not yet perceived or understood.

"A threshold is not a simple boundary," writes John O'Donohue, "it is a frontier that divides two different territories, rhythms, and atmospheres."[3]

In the world of nature, the chrysalis is such a frontier, the space between two territories where neither the caterpillar nor the butterfly has form or shape. Liminal.

For almost forty days, we inhabit liminal space, we live a chrysalis life, our days a helpless hanging on.

Recovering from radiation therapy proves to be as tricky and unpredictable as recovering from brain surgery. Since both have occurred within six months, it's double jeopardy. "It takes years for the brain to recover," I hear Schneider say.

The journey is painfully slow, one step forward and two steps back. Most days, Nate experiences energy—surges in the day that last from thirty minutes to an hour, then he's flat on the couch, struggling to keep his eyelids open.

During an energy surge, he and I go for a drive to break up the day. Sometimes he can hold a conversation, other times we drive in silence. I can't help but wonder if he is listless because of the treatment, or if this is the cancer taking over.

---

2. Alexander et al, "Liminal Space," 18.

3. O'Donohue, *To Bless the Space*, 48.

*Stay in hope. Be here. Try not to look over the edge of today.*

"I feel like I'm regressing," Nate says toward the end of January, two weeks out of treatment.

"Not according to the green sheet," I say.

Together we look at the one-page summary from CancerCare: *Caring for Yourself After Radiation Treatment.*

"The tiredness and fatigue will continue while your body heals," says the green sheet. "Your energy levels will return with time, usually within eight to twelve weeks after your last day of treatment."

The green sheet, however, says nothing about the emotional recovery after radiation: how the burns on the skin get branded on the heart; how the wounds in the psyche are as cumulative as the radiation in the brainstem.

An image comes to Nate in the wee hours of the morning. He is on a deserted dirt road. The trees on either side of the road are barren, their trunks and twigs as still as lifeless sentinels. The sky overhead is dark and threatening. He is walking alone. He asks Jesus to walk with him on this stretch. He hears nothing.

"God is gone," he says.

"Who was that guy who spoke about God in the video at church? Who was that guy who was so confident about battling a brain tumor?" he asks, his tone scathing. "That guy mocks me day and night."

I'm silent, unsure how to respond. Have I not journeyed to these same places in my own heart? Disillusioned. Bitterly complaining to God for allowing my son to go through this hell? Have I not cried out in the night: "The tumor was supposed to be benign! How long, O Lord, how long must he suffer? Have mercy on him, heal him. And if he's not healed . . . don't let him suffer long."

I wonder about the dream then, and about Schneider's words of hope. Are signs and dreams meant for the day? Are they meant for a season? Will the hope of the dream hold? I don't know. How can I? How can any of us? Is it any less a mercy if it doesn't?

I write an e-mail update to the community.

"We are in the long middle," I say, "where loneliness is a constant companion, consolation cannot be found, and faith is brittle."

The long middle. This is liminal space.


IN 2011, AT AGE twenty-one, Nate was among the more than 8,000 young adults in Canada[4] to hear the words *you have cancer.* Yet this demographic

---

4. Young Adult Cancer Canada, "Our History," line 17.

of patients has been largely overlooked by the Canadian cancer care system designed to help them.

But that is changing, thanks to a groundbreaking report.

But first, allow me to return to a scene from our story.

The hematology waiting area at downtown Winnipeg's CancerCare was overflowing with people. It was December 27, 2011. Like the rest of the city, the lab located in the atrium of the building was closed for the Christmas holidays, resulting in a backlog of cancer patients in need of bloodwork. Cancer never takes a holiday, nor do the chemotherapy treatments designed to halt its advance.

Fortunately, Norm, Nate, and I found a place to sit together on the expansive brick border that surrounded the garden at the far end of the room. The chairs were all taken, except for a few random singles here and there. Six weeks deep into treatment, Nate knew the weekly drill. He presented himself at the brain tumor clinic, next door to hematology, and produced his health card.

"Your full name and date of birth?" the receptionist asked. The answer to this question was the secret password to receive the necessary requisition form.

Sheet in hand, Nate proceeded to hematology and took a number. Today, he was number eighty-five. His oncologist was keeping a keen eye on his platelet count. Temozolomide, the chemotherapy drug Nate was taking, had a nasty reputation for destroying platelets in the body beyond what was considered helpful.

Looking around the room, I noticed a startling disparity. Most of the people in the chairs were middle-aged and older; most of the hair that glistened in the natural light from surrounding windows was gray in color. Yes, there was the odd young person, but she was usually accompanying a patient, clutching that sheet of paper. Inside these walls, the requisition form was the great leveler.

At twenty-one, Nate was out of place in this crowd. He belonged neither to the pediatric group of cancer patients getting their blood tested elsewhere in the building, nor to the older adult population surrounding us. At twenty-one, Nate fell squarely in the gap between two monumental cancer care systems in our country.

That gap was exposed in April 2017 when the Canadian Partnership Against Cancer, an agency commissioned by the federal government, released a report called *Adolescents and Young Adults with Cancer in Canada*.

The news was not good.

According to the report, adolescents and young adults with cancer (AYAs, as they're referred to in the report) are "substantially under-represented in cancer research in Canada."[5] AYAs are studied much less than other patient subsets in this country, such as pediatric or older adults with cancer.

"While total investment in Canadian cancer research has increased over time," says the study, "the proportion of funding allocated to adolescent and young-adult-specific research has changed little from 2005 to 2013."[6]

The evidence is clear: significant gaps in knowledge and care exist for this important demographic in Canada.

For a group on the cusp of adulthood—most with underdeveloped coping skills—the news is particularly tragic. Rites of passage such as higher education studies and career launches, romantic relationships, and the beginning of independent living are all but demolished by the cancer experience, resulting in a lifelong struggle for those who survive. Perhaps most devastating, certainly in the short-term, is the isolation—the disconnection from peers.

In her 2014 book, *This Should Not be Happening to Me: Young Adults With Cancer*, former Winnipeg therapist Anne Katz says, "Most young adults live under the canopy of the three I's: invulnerability, immortality, and invincibility. Life-threatening illnesses happen to older people, not to their friends and peers."[7]

This was certainly true for Nate, diagnosed with brain cancer halfway through his business administration degree. The independence that was within his grasp evaporated during his season of maximum-strength radiation and chemotherapy treatments.

Day-to-day survival eclipsed any dreams for the future. Activities he took for granted—driving, studying, working out, even sleeping—were stripped from him, leaving him completely dependent on his family. And the psychological and physiological toll from surgery and treatment meant that *if* and *when* he reentered studies, it would be at a diminished capacity.

Nate's friends struggled to relate to his illness, never mind the possibility that he could die from the disease. The isolation and loneliness he experienced was crushing.

Add to that the issue of fertility, and the way forward becomes even more complex. Many of the chemotherapies administered to this demographic destroy their ability to have a family.

5. Canadian Partnership Against Cancer, "Adolescents & Young Adults," 11.

6. Canadian Partnership Against Cancer, "Adolescents & Young Adults," 11.

7. Katz, *This Should Not Be Happening*, 167.

What's clear from the study is that we *can* and *should* do more for this demographic.

"Research specifically focused on the AYA age group," concludes the study, "can help the cancer control community understand the unique biology of AYA cancers and the unique needs—sexual and reproductive health, psychological care, and survivorship needs—of AYAs with cancer, which can inform the development of interventions to improve cancer care and to support the lifelong care needs of AYA cancer survivors."[8]

I hope change comes soon. For the more than 8,000 young men and women who hear the news *you have cancer* this year, their lives may depend on it.

Here's what I know: there are few people in any relationship circle who dare to walk the long middle; or stand in the tragic gap; or inhabit liminal space. It is simply too emotionally demanding, too painful, too time-consuming and, quite honestly, too terrifying. There are many who show up for the beginning and the end, but few can look at suffering for long. Ask anyone with a serious illness; ask anyone who is suffering with a cancer diagnosis when the prognosis is grim. People flee.

Our society does not know what to do with sick people. We don't know how to hold them. Arms-length please, or preferably from a distance. But up close? No, thank you!

"Please text or call if you need anything at all," is a common response. Polite, thoughtful in the abstract. But completely unhelpful because it puts the burden of response back onto the sufferer. People in crisis don't have the energy or even the awareness of what they need apart from day-to-day survival.

It's far more helpful to be concrete. Offer to bring a meal on a specific day, provide a ride to radiation appointments, shovel snow or mow the lawn.

There are reasons we stay at a distance. We are, after all, citizens of the first, or Minority World, where we trust the rational systems of government, commerce, and social life, where even nature bends to our wishes. These constructs have proved reliable.

"We are bothered by the inexplicable and uncontrollable," says Susan Phillips, "viewing disease, disaster, and death as crises that are, in large part, subject to our control."[9]

---

8. Canadian Partnership Against Cancer, "Adolescents & Young Adults," 13.

9. Phillips, *Candlelight*, 99.

Phillips calls it our "visceral theology,"[10] even though we know there is no evidence in the scriptural narrative that says the faithful are spared suffering.

This visceral theology gets in the way of holding one another well. As if suffering is somehow contagious. As if contact will mess with how we understand the "formula" for blessing: "If I pray correctly and am a good person, then God will have to reward me with life, liberty, and the acquisition of wealth."

Of course, we would never say this out loud, or even admit it to ourselves. Entitlement is embedded in our bones. We say we don't define blessed-ness by health, freedom, or the size of our bank accounts. We go to great lengths to criticize groups that do. "Prosperity gospel," we mutter under our breath while flipping the channels on the remote, pausing to hear the latest pronouncements from some celebrity preacher with a megawatt smile.

But somewhere deep down, don't we believe a version of this, too? "Maybe," we say to ourselves in secret, "if I check all the boxes, I'll get a pass." It is a distortion deeply rooted in our humanity. Visceral.

"We're enjoying life to the full right now; we're blessed," we say in casual conversation. "My wife got a promotion; we're blessed." We post pictures of our Mexican vacation on social media. #Blessed. This has now become the new and not-so-subtle way of boasting. "Look at me. I'm so lucky. #Blessed."

The word is threadbare with overuse and empty of meaning. It's seductive to believe that success equals blessing. But it's a dangerous equation. What then do we do with pain and adversity? Do they indicate the opposite? Do they indicate the absence of God? Or worse, his curse?

"Blessed are those who mourn; blessed are the poor in spirit," says Jesus in the Gospel according to St. Matthew. Those in the New Testament who were closest to divinity and blessed by their proximity and affinity to Christ were his disciples. Yet they more often experienced poverty, duress, homelessness, exhaustion, and, in most cases, a premature and violent death. There is nothing in their story about ease, comfort, or material things. This gospel—this *good* news—runs counter to our deepest North American convictions.

Helplessness gets in the way, too. What do we say when there are no easy answers? When science doesn't come through? What do we say when we can't say or do something to "fix" others? What do we say when we can't explain God?

10. Phillips, *Candlelight*, 99.

Most of us possess a strong compulsion to be God's advocate, God's defender, God's public relations representative. When the cancer appears terminal, when prayer has all but dried up, mystery, questions, and doubt are tenuous propositions.

During such times, we need a trustworthy friend who knows what it means to simply receive and bear witness to our pain. Sometimes these friends are the same people we've always turned to for support. Often they are not.

Meet Harry and Liz. They showed up on our doorstep the week of Nate's cancer diagnosis in late November. Nate had never met them before. I knew them only as the parents of a friend, who, as it turned out, encouraged the two of them to visit us in our desperate hour.

Harry was a warrior. Nine years earlier, when he was in his early sixties and the picture of health, Harry was diagnosed with advanced leukemia and given two weeks to live. But God had other plans. Harry survived every treatment—chemotherapy, radiation, a bone marrow transplant—and was now undergoing experimental therapies. Harry was astonishing the North American medical community with his resilience.

"Stay in your story," Harry insisted when we complained about some people's annoying habit of parroting appalling cancer stories in the face of Nate's diagnosis, like it was some sort of cancer competition.

"Stay in your story" became our mantra.

"Don't resist the radiation beams, Nate," said Harry, "receive them." It was Harry who first dubbed the radiation mask the "helmet of salvation."

Had the angel Gabriel dressed himself in human form that day, he may have looked a lot like Harry. He appeared to us with a slightly worn and wizened face, crowned with a surprising head of dark hair and moustache to match. And while Harry did not say "fear not" in so many words, his message to receive rather than resist sounded like something from a divine handbook, delivered by an unmistakably clear voice with an undeniably steady gaze.

Harry and Liz had hung out in liminal space for nine years and now invited us into their experience. They were veterans of waiting. After Harry's cancer diagnosis, they retired to their family cottage in a lake community an hour out of the city. Nate and I visited them there in the weeks following Nate's treatment.

We never talked about cancer. Instead, Harry and Nate ventured into the woods with their walking sticks while the elder explained every fold of nature, identifying the oldest tree in the forest or pointing out the remnants of an eagle's nest. They also played shinny at the local hockey rink, Harry feeding Nate one-timers. Their shared suffering was a silent companion.

Once, when I grumbled to Liz about people who had vanished since the cancer diagnosis, she said simply, "Friends become acquaintances, and acquaintances become friends."

Her words stayed with me. Anger and frustration had blinded me to the community that was shaping under my nose. Yes, this community included longtime friends like Cheryl, Mary, Vic, Willy, Warren and Sandy, along with our extended families. But our community was also growing to include people who were acquainted with suffering like Harry, Liz, and Randy. And, in particular, it included those who were well acquainted with suffering alongside a child with cancer like Jeannette and Elmer.

This was our liminal community. These were the ones who braved our precarious frontier.

God's mercy. It slips in beside you while you're busy looking the other direction.

"We have the right complement of people in our lives right now," I wrote to a friend in early February. "This is pure provision. God has prepared a table before us in the presence of this enemy, this cancer. And he has placed you around it."

This is the secret of liminal community that no one can tell you until the worst happens. There is a table. There are people who come. And those who show up just might surprise you.

Henry, from Nigeria, certainly did.

# 12

# Henry

We are moving through deep space and we can't, for the life of us, comprehend how we keep moving forward in such a paralyzing story. Yet we do. Each day arrives and we rise to it. Mysteriously. This motion can only be called grace. All other words fail to hold our capacity to put one foot in front of the other.

—Jan's journal, February 13, 2012

The last name on my call display was familiar, even though I failed, time and again, to pronounce it correctly. I smiled and quickly picked up.

"Hello," I said.

"Hi Jan, it's Henry. How is Nathan? How are his spirits?"

In his typical endearing manner, Henry wasted no time getting to the point. It was the second full week of February.

The last time we had met together was in mid-December, halfway through Nate's treatment, just two weeks after Henry's prayer shook the walls of our family gathering. Nate had agreed to see Henry, even though the meeting would take place in the evening when Nate usually felt most exhausted.

On that visit, Henry explained how praying for our son had become something of an occupation; that, often, in the wee hours of the morning, he would pace the floor of the prayer furnace, talking with God, wrestling with him, asking him to spare Nate's life.

I was dumbfounded. *Who does this for a stranger? Who goes without sleep for someone he doesn't even know?*

Henry did.

"Can I come and pray with Nathan on Wednesday afternoon?"

Wednesday afternoon—February 15—two days before Nate's MRI, the red-letter day we had been anticipating and dreading. We were living the countdown, marking off the hours, measuring time in teaspoons, waiting for the picture that would tell us how to live or die.

"Really?" I answered cautiously. "You want to come to our home?"

Didn't he know this was a dangerous time to breathe our air, to see our unveiled grief, to look into our swollen eyes, to dare intercede for our perilous circumstances? Didn't he know? Wasn't he afraid or just a little scared?

"Yes, we would very much like that," I heard myself say in a tone that held both surprise and excitement. "See you Wednesday."

As I SHUFFLED THROUGH papers on Wednesday morning, I glanced at it. There it was—forgotten. Dead. The remnant of a friend's care.

It was an orchid, perched on the edge of my desk. I had seen its sad form so many times over the past weeks, each time vowing to put it in the trash.

Three months ago, I had made a decision, probably more subconscious than deliberate. I would stop watering it. Grief will do that. It will sabotage small kindnesses, like watering a plant. My world had collapsed into malignant sadness and, with it, my commitment to nurture a flowerless orchid.

The plant was now a study in neglect: two oversized, yellow leaves; exposed, gnarled roots; a brittle, brown twig shooting upward, with a cobweb sagging pitifully from it.

I didn't see it at first, the secret that newly dangled from the twig. It had formed when I wasn't watching, when I didn't care.

Yet, there it hung: a bulb.

It was purple, the size of a quarter, attached by the thinnest thread to the twig I had assumed was dead. What had been said to that flower bulb to make it come forth? Who was the Sayer? What did it mean?

"You won't believe this," I yelled from the study.

Nate was visiting with a friend downstairs when I burst into their conversation, plant in hand.

"Look!" I said, pointing to the ball hanging precariously, "It's alive."

The two of them stared at me, confused, likely concerned about my mental health. I must have sounded ridiculous, my excitement gushing like a geyser into their otherwise serious conversation.

But that bulb! That delicate bulb held the mystery of the universe for me. It was an unexpected mercy that flowered out of barrenness: undeserved, unearned—like redemption, like salvation.

Somewhere in the land of the forgotten and neglected, I felt God's gaze.

"Keep watch my soul," it seemed to say. "Find me in the hidden places, in the quiet workings of time and grace."

Henry arrives, a well-worn Bible in hand.

"Hello, Nathan, my friend," he says in his thick, melodic accent. The two of them embrace.

I have forgotten that Nate stands head and shoulders above Henry. I have forgotten how the light reflects off Henry's broad smile through the space between his two front teeth. I have forgotten that Henry insists on using Nate's full name, Nathan.

He greets us warmly, speaking softly and carrying a certain lightness, a joviality even.

"I'm praying and fasting for Nathan," he reports after settling into the red chair in our living room. "If it's okay, I would like to come to your home for the next four days to pray with you."

If it's okay with us? "Yes, yes!" I want to shout. "You had me at *fasting*." But I manage to be a little less dramatic, to tame my full-blown shock. "Yes, please come and pray with us. We would be so grateful."

Henry's kindness overwhelms me. He doesn't know us. He is, by all accounts, a stranger. Yet he's fasting and praying for us. It's the kind of prayer that goes without food—for days—as a way to hear God's voice over the din of the world, as a way to stay open to wonder.

Very few people on the planet are holding to this level of commitment on our behalf. But, to this short list, we can now add the man before us: Henry.

Henry and his family have been in Canada barely a year. All I know about Henry is that he spent most of his life in Nigeria working as a pastor in a country where many Christians face daily scorn and hatred.

Henry's Nigeria is one of the most dangerous countries in the world to be a follower of Christ. As the most populous nation in Africa, Nigeria is home to nearly 200 million people, divided between a majority-Christian south and a majority-Muslim north. Hundreds of Christians are killed each month by militant groups: men, women, children—whole villages.

Hundreds of people, big and small, are slaughtered because of their faith. It is alarming and utterly disturbing. The air they breathe is toxic, full of fear, anxiety, and threat of repeated trauma. It is high, the price they pay to identify as believers.

After living a life plundered by unrest and persecution, Henry has been stripped of everything but God. Maybe that's why he lives on prayer. Maybe that's what makes him fierce.

We talk for a time about gospel stories, about Jesus healing the man born blind, helping his disciples learn that human suffering isn't always about personal sin.

"Did he sin or did his parents?" the disciples ask. "Neither," Jesus says, "this is a moment to reveal God's glory." And he heals the man right on the spot.

We talk, too, about the Lazarus story, when Jesus comes too late to the funeral of his friend, then raises him back to life as evidence of God's in-breaking glory.

"I believe God wants to show his glory in Nate," says Henry.

Henry is a Pentecostal believer, a branch of Christianity that, in Nigeria, has exploded with growth in recent decades. The Pentecostal movement, born in the late nineteenth century, emphasizes baptism of the Holy Spirit, evidenced by speaking in tongues, prophecy, and healing of mind, body, and spirit.

Many North Americans have come to associate Pentecostalism with television preachers with megawatt smiles, high on the fumes of a prosperity gospel, flitting across the continent in private jets. But this can distort the fuller truth about a group of God's people who are upsetting systems—spiritual, social, and political—and transforming the planet for the common good.

I recognize Henry's unvarnished zeal. When I was in my mid-twenties, I attended a healing conference in Winnipeg sponsored by the Vineyard, a group of Christians who believe something similar. My curiosity, my desire to discover more about faith from these people who hold that God in Christ is still in-breaking on the natural order of things, urged me to attend.

I also came with my own quiet desperation. For six years, I had suffered with urinary tract infections (UTIs) that left me on a merry-go-round of monthly antibiotics. While my condition was not life-threatening, it was debilitating as I struggled to raise a toddler and baby at twenty-five.

After one teaching session, the speaker instructed attendees to request prayer for healing by reaching out to someone nearby. I did. A woman put her hand on my abdomen and prayed to undo the doctor's words that I would need to "live with this condition."

How did she know? In our brief exchange, I hadn't told her. Then she prayed for the power of the Holy Spirit to move through my body and touch the affected area. Something like fire began to course through my body, an unusual heat, causing me to drip with sweat. And then it was over. I went home and told Norm.

What happened after that was nothing short of a miracle for me. The UTIs became less frequent, giving my body a chance to build up its own resistance. The cycle was broken.

Now, some twenty years later, I'm looking into Henry's charismatic face and see my own reflection. True, the shape of my faith has become more ancient, more liturgical, spacious with mystery: I pray the Divine Hours, I recite the creeds, I carry prayer beads in my purse.

Yet, some part of me has always been Pentecostal; always believed that God in Christ cannot be tamed by reason and logic, that he does not fit into a tidy set of propositions, that he is quite possibly wild beyond my comprehension. Wild with love, wild with goodness.

This mystery unites us, courses through our veins like oxygen, no matter our denomination, no matter our tradition. This truth binds us together as the "holy catholic Church."

"Sift through the history of the church and find the *Yes of God*," my favorite seminary professor used to say.

At its best, the Pentecostal movement is the *Yes of God*, reclaiming what Catholic scholar and theologian Francis MacNutt refers to as the "full heritage of healing" that has always been part of the 2,000-year-old community that calls itself Christian.[1]

Still, I struggle to believe it here and now in this diagnosis, with the impossible occupying a place in Nate's brainstem. Despite my own experience of healing several decades earlier, it is hard to harness my doubts.

I analyze Henry's words, his methods, his theology. I ask a lot of questions. Despite Henry's kindness, there is a tiny skeptic inside of me, skittishly scanning the horizon of his faith to make sure he's for real.

What if he's a fanatic, a snake-oil-touting-counterfeit? How would we know? For months, Norm and I have shielded Nate from people's probing questions ("What's your prognosis?"), from their absurd comments ("My second cousin was diagnosed with a brain tumor and he's palliative"), and from their unwelcome germs and bacteria.

Should we be shielding him now from Henry?

"I am only a man," says Henry, as he bends over Nate to pray. "Our gaze must remain fixed on Jesus, our intercessor. His touch has the power

---

1. MacNutt, *Healing*, 40.

to make Nathan well, not my words. Lord, mercifully heal Nathan," he says with vigor, with tenderness, again and again, as if the boy in front of him were his son.

Tears are dripping off my face, pooling in my lap and I can't stop them. Underneath all my suspicions, my layers of doubt, I feel something else.

It is visceral, deep down in my gut, below the premonitions in my reptilian brain. It is *love*. It is love that flows from Jesus to Henry, a tide that leaves me breathless. It is humbling to experience this from a stranger, to be the recipient of this kind of love, gutted by the side of the road and bandaged by a Samaritan.

Henry is humble. Henry believes. He knows his human limitations and to whom he prays. His belief that God in Christ is able stirs in us long after the man leaves an hour later. Faith inflates.

Henry knows Nate's diagnosis; he is well aware of the drastic medical interventions Nate has experienced and the probable outcomes. The vigor of the scientific community is not lost on him.

Yet he approaches prayer with equal vigor. He gives himself entirely and unequivocally to the One-in-Three, the Three-in-One. I am astonished that he possesses such an unshakeable grip on the belief that this Trinity ultimately has the final word.

How Henry's faith blooms with so much color and vitality out of Nigeria's wasteland is a mystery to me. Like my orchid.

THE DAY OF NATE's MRI has finally arrived. It will happen at seven o'clock this evening. The day stretches out before us like the endless snow-covered fields we pass on our drive.

Henry comes to our home for the third time in as many days. Yesterday morning, he stayed only ten minutes to pray. This afternoon, we invite Jeannette and Elmer to join us. They, too, are keeping vigil with a faith formed by a decade of living among African Christians in Burkina Faso, a neighboring country to Nigeria. They will help us discern and hear God through Henry.

Today, Henry employs some unconventional methods.

"Can you remove your socks, Nathan?" he asks.

Henry begins by placing his hands on Nate's feet, his knees, his torso, until his hand are cupping Nate's head.

"Break the yoke," he repeats loudly, firmly, evenly. There is a heaviness that Nate carries, explains Henry.

"Set him free," he commands. "Separate this heavy yoke from Nathan. Free him of it."

"Yes, and amen," we say together. "Yes, and amen."

Living with a brain tumor is burdensome, suffocating. Nate desires to be free. He desires to be separated from its oppression.

That evening, the three of us sit together for what would become another ritual at three-month intervals: waiting for the MRI technician to call Nate's name. Nate would be injected with a contrast dye before lying in a tube of spinning magnets that would buzz and knock around his head.

Norm and I would pass the time praying silently—Norm in the direction of the television screen, and me thumbing the small, wooden prayer beads and cross that ring around my index finger. *Lord, have mercy.*

The ride home is quiet, our fate set in motion. The map of Nate's brain will tell our story. Tomorrow, a radiologist will know. And six days later, so will we.

Tonight, we celebrate by treating Nate to a venti chocolate chip Frappuccino, double-blended, sugar be damned.

The next afternoon, Henry arrives for his fourth and final time of prayer. Today, Laura is present.

He enters in his usual quiet, unassuming way. But something is different. Henry appears fidgety, slightly excited, awkward even, like a young man about to drop down on one knee and propose, but unsure how to go about it.

As he climbs the stairs to our living room and settles into what has unofficially become *his* red chair, he looks from Nate to Norm to Laura to me, and asks, "Did any of you hear anything since yesterday—did you hear anything from God?"

Silence.

The three of us look from one to the other, blinking. We return his gaze, confused.

"What do you mean?" Norm finally asks.

"Well," he says slowly, deliberately, "while I was praying last night, I heard God say that Nathan is healed."

More silence. Stupefied silence.

Henry repeats the news again, making full eye contact with each of us. He doesn't flinch. He doesn't stutter. He speaks clearly, plainly.

Later, a month from now, he would tell me he could barely look at me because of what he saw in my eyes: daggers, a mama bear about to maul. It must have been frightening, chilling, the face I instinctively wore, my face of fierce protection.

He would tell me that his wife, a palliative care nurse, had cautioned him. "Henry, after all that family has been through, are you really going to walk in there and tell them this news? You better be sure."

In the forty-five minutes that follow, we talk about faith, that amorphous quality that defines what it means to be a Christian, to take a risk on God, despite the odds, despite having medical evidence to the contrary. Henry opens his well-worn Bible to Romans 4, which recounts the story of Abraham and Sarah, the couple who become parents in their old age, when all human ability to reproduce is long dead.

"It was hard for me to come into your home and speak this word," he says. "But I chose not to be timid. *Nathan, you are healed*," he says again, his words punctuated by raw conviction.

My body is covered in goosebumps. I look at Norm. Our eyes meet and we exchange a wordless glance reflecting shades of . . . what exactly? Worry, fear. Doubt? Nate is sitting between us on the couch, his body slumped and head down.

*Dear God, what now?*

"Be bold, Nathan," says Henry pleadingly, his gaze fixed on Nate. "Don't hold back! Receive this word into your heart. Bind yourself to it. Open your mouth so God can fill it."

Silence.

Suddenly, Nate sits forward, his body stiff, face taut, as his words tumble out.

"It's hard for me, you know," he says between sobs, his hands gesturing wildly. "It's so hard to speak because of how things went after my last report. *It hurt so bad*."

There it was, that gaping wound that split our hearts into *before* and *after*.

"He speaks!" Henry shouts, erupting in laughter.

"Don't shut up, Nathan. Don't give the devil any reason to think you've surrendered. God is strengthening you through all this adversity. But you must open your mouth—you must speak out what you believe. Don't surrender to fear."

Laura speaks. "I believe Nate is healed," she says with confidence. Her courage amazes me. She doesn't wait for anyone else in the room. She doesn't care what we think. She's willing to throw herself headlong into this declaration. Henry squeals with laughter and delight.

Some part of me feels like I'm watching this scene from a distance, out of body. I'm oddly perturbed. The air in our home is wrapped in a solemn fog, has been for weeks. Henry's raucous laughter rips through it, a spirited hymn in the middle of a funeral dirge. It's inappropriate, untimely, rude even. If he perceives my wordless reproach, he doesn't let on.

In the meantime, Kate walks in the front door. She takes a place around the circle.

My eyes are on Nate, though. He seems visibly shaken.

"In the MRI machine, I talked with God," says Nate with tears. "I asked for healing, I asked God to change the picture of barrenness into springtime goodness. But it was quiet in there, except for the knocking sounds around me."

Nate hesitates, wipes his nose with his sleeve and looks at Kate. "I'm glad you're here," he says. "I want you to hear this."

"The woman—the technician—slides me out of the machine. I take out my earplugs and swing my legs over the side of the gurney and fiddle with my hospital gown. I'm trying to hurry, to piece myself back together.

"When I reach down for my shoes, I hear a voice that says, *By the grace of God, you are healed.* This voice, this word—it, like, sideswipes me. Stops me short. I keep thinking it can't be coming from me—I'm too busy trying to get myself out of the machine, too busy organizing myself to manufacture a word like that."

"*By the grace of God, you are healed*," Nate says again, this time slowly, listening to each syllable, letting the words wash over him.

The tears are spilling fast and Nate takes a moment to wipe them away before continuing. "I wasn't going to say anything," he looks at me and Norm, his face swollen, eyes rimmed red, "because I was afraid of being hurt again. But after what Henry said when he first arrived, I knew I couldn't—I didn't want to—keep quiet."

"My God!" says Henry, his eyes shining. "I'm confirming what you heard!"

"And *when* did you hear this word?" asks Henry, his body leaning forward, his voice earnest.

"Around 8:30 p.m., I guess," says Nate. "Right after my MRI."

Silence.

Now it's Henry's turn to be dumbfounded. Shaking his head, he says, "That's exactly the time God told me you were healed."

We would find out later that Henry had prayed for this, prayed that if this was God's word over Nate, that Nate would hear it, too. That he did hear it—and at the same time, no less—filled the man with a sense of wonder, a wonder that began its slow rise in our own hearts.

I don't know what to think, what to say. It's not that I don't believe, that I have given up hope. It's just that my faith is stripped of any kind of certainty. We have lived these months making room for all the possibilities. Now, I am downright terrified of being disappointed again.

Could we be *in* on a holy secret? There is new life dangling by the thinnest of threads on the branches of all that is dead in us.

Five days from now we will know for sure.

# 13

## Gone

No, he is too quick. We never
catch him at it. He is there
sooner than our thought or prayer.
Searching backward, we cannot discover
*how*, or get inside the miracle.

—Luci Shaw[1]

It is 1:30 p.m. on Friday, February 24. The three of us are sitting in one of the tiny clinic rooms that ring around the brain tumor clinic at CancerCare. We are waiting for the door to open, waiting for the five-minute conversation that will tilt our world toward life or death.

Science will scrutinize Henry's prophetic word and test its truth. Will the word prevail? Suddenly, under these lights, within these walls, it feels freakishly far-fetched.

*God, will we prevail if, somehow, we've heard wrong?*

"They all know," I think to myself, white coats brushing past us as we move to an examination room barely big enough to hold three chairs and a small bed.

All the oncologists, neurosurgeons, pharmacists, nurses, and support staff have met together that morning to review each patient's results. It

1. Shaw, *Accompanied by Angels*, 79.

is their Friday ritual. Together, they analyze every MRI, read aloud each radiation report, devise the next treatment plan, and plot the way forward.

When the first patient arrives at one o'clock, the team members are ready to make their entrance, playing their part in what must be, most Fridays, a carousel of heartbreak.

I don't know how they do it.

Norm and I sit on either side of Nate, our hands clasped tightly, our bodies straining to hold the tension that has devoured our appetite and stolen our sleep. Raw energy pulsates through us, wordless and wired, caged in a question.

Henry's word echoes through our thoughts; it is lodged deep in our hearts, too holy to share beyond our circle of six. It has kept us steady.

Our request to family and close friends reads: "Please uphold us in this holy moment with your prayers—that the medical evidence would point to the healing touch of God in Nate's brainstem, that Nate would be granted newness of life in the land of the living. We trust that our help comes from the Lord, the Maker of heaven and earth, that he will always have the final word on our son's days . . . but our hearts tremble."

Laura and Kate have taken time off work to join us this afternoon. They sit in the waiting room at the front of the clinic. The stress of this moment manifests itself differently in each girl. Laura sits quietly, pensive, tissue in hand, while Kate chats and laughs with the CancerCare volunteers who offer her apple juice and cookies from their cart.

Kelly, our oncologist nurse, is the first to come through the door. By my estimation, Kelly is in her mid-forties. She is fit and attractive with piercing blue eyes, a bright presence, incongruous with her surroundings. Today, her long, blond hair is in a ponytail.

Clipboard in hand, she sits directly across from Nate. Following standard procedure, Kelly peruses Nate's responses to questions from the intake form that he filled out when he first arrived. "On a scale of one to ten, do you experience body pain? Do you have an appetite? Do you feel depressed?"

I search her face for any trace of knowing, for a slight smile, a flicker of warmth in those penetrating blue eyes, anything that might give me a clue as to what she heard earlier. We all know better than to ask her outright about the results. Her role is to ask another series of questions on yet another checklist, to provide a sketch of Nate's wellness for Dr. Schneider.

"Any tingling in your hands or feet?" she asks.

"No," says Nate.

"Any trouble with balance or walking?"

"No."

"Any prolonged headaches or change to your vision?" she asks.

"No."

"What about numbness—is there any numbness on one side of your body?"

"No," Nate says again, his one knee bobbing up and down in an agitated rhythm.

"Okay," Kelly finally says, seemingly satisfied as she gets up to leave. "Dr. Schneider will be with you shortly."

Our breath catches. The moment brings us closer. We listen more carefully to the sounds in the hallway, hearing footsteps and bits of muffled conversation. How long will we wait?

The door closes in the next clinic room and we hear what seems to be Dr. Schneider's voice. Another patient? How many of us are waiting in these rooms for a pronouncement, in this place where there are no cures, where most news sends you reeling on another winding roller coaster ride.

Suddenly, the door opens and Dr. Schneider appears, his white coat hanging drably off his frame as usual, sleeves rolled up, and a piece of paper waving from his hand.

*Finally!*

"You've had a remarkable response to the treatment," he says excitedly, quickly closing the door and standing over us.

We sit up straight now, completely leaning into his presence. This is Schneider's way—direct, no preamble, leading with results. While other doctors amble into the room, page through their files and ask annoying questions like, "How are you feeling?"—such a cruel form of torture!— Schneider announces his news bluntly, knowing it is the only thing that matters to his patients.

Sitting down, Schneider traces his index finger along a phrase in the last paragraph of the radiation report.

"The tumor has virtually disappeared," he reads, shaking his head, a smile playing at the edge of his mouth, as if he's been shaking his head and repeating the news to himself all morning.

"It's just so remarkable."

Gasps escape, rippling relief through our bodies, as we struggle to comprehend. We cannot speak, muzzled by shock. We can only look at one another with wide smiles and misty eyes.

"I'll tell you something," says Schneider incredulously. "When we saw those MRI slides today, my team kept looking back and forth between the *before* and *after* images to make sure we had the right identification on the skull.

"Because the tumor cloud is gone!"

These six simple words are the winged promise of a future.

Silence.

"Would you say this is in the category of . . . a miracle?" I finally ask, my voice barely above a whisper.

"Well," Schneider muses, measuring his words carefully. "I can't remember the last time I saw a report like this. And this radiologist," he says, pointing to the name on the bottom of the report, "is one of the best. I've never seen him use a word like *disappear*. It's just not in his vocabulary.

"To be honest with you folks, I'm blown away by the results."

"Oh, God," Norm groans.

It is eight minutes into the appointment, a full eight minutes of shock and awe. And just like that, the conversation shifts, and we're back to the business of cancer.

"The next step," explains Schneider, "is to ensure the area is swept completely clean, to guarantee that any remaining residue is obliterated. And for that, we will administer six rounds of chemotherapy for the next six months at double the dose of temozolomide that Nate was receiving during radiation. We'll begin next Wednesday."

"Sure," says Nate mechanically. We nod in agreement, not caring what will happen five days from now. Not caring that the proposed chemotherapy regimen is double the dose. It could have been tripled and we wouldn't have batted an eyelash at that moment.

What matters most, what pulses through every breath, every thought, is the word *disappeared*. We are lost in its glory. We are free-falling into wonder.

Schneider excuses himself from the room and advises us to wait for the pharmacist.

Norm jumps to his feet. "I'm telling the girls!" he says, already running down the hall. Laura sobs with relief and Kate is high-fiving her dad and anyone else she can find.

Nate and I exchange a hug, wiping tears, oblivious to all else. Shortly after Norm returns, the pharmacist for the brain tumor clinic makes her appearance. She's a tall, dark-eyed, dark-haired beauty with short bangs and straight white teeth.

"Congratulations on the good news, Nate," she says, all smiles. "You have had a complete response to treatment, something we rarely see in this clinic. Now, we want to build on the good work and make sure the area remains clean."

Again, we nod in dazed agreement.

The pharmacist quickly picks up where Schneider left off, enthusiastically moving through the plan, detailing how and when the 350 milligrams of temozolomide will be administered, outlining the potential risks as a brisk afterthought. We sit spellbound, too preoccupied to protest, dazzled by those teeth, that smile, and the sheer volume of information coming at us.

"Also, we need to address the problem of your suppressed blood cell production and this particular chemotherapy. I understand you experienced myelosuppression in the last weeks of your combined temozolomide/radiation treatment?"

"Yes," says Nate.

"So, to counteract that problem, we prescribe a drug called Neupogen. This medication helps your body make more white blood cells, which, as you know, are important to help you fight off infections. Many people using Neupogen do not have serious side effects. Some patients experience mild bone pain, but that's unusual," she says with a shrug.

Silence.

"We will give you nine injections after each round of chemotherapy, just above the belly button," she continues. "For now, we will make arrangements for a home care nurse to administer the shots. But we could certainly train you in the future," she says brightly, looking at me.

I stare at her wide-eyed, unblinking, and shake my head no.

When we finally exit CancerCare, the five of us walk through the double doors into the February sunshine, our future changed. Nate will be alive to celebrate his twenty-second birthday in June. We want to shout, to sing at the top of our lungs, to fall to our knees on the sidewalk and say "thank you" over and over again until our throats go dry.

Instead, we walk giddily through the parking lot, praying our gratitudes in the car.

Later that afternoon, we share the news, first with our dear ones, and then with our e-mail community.

*We are experiencing a great deal of shock and awe, knowing the joy that arrived in our hearts today will explode into celebration in the days to come. By the grace of God, Nate has been healed. We are humbled by the mercy God has poured out on our son.*

Somewhere during that time, I call Henry. He squeals with delight. "Jesus, thank you, Jesus!" I hear him cry. "I am dancing," he shouts into the phone.

"I am dancing and I cannot stop!"

# 14

## Wonder

**The Widow of Nain**

I am she
Though not a widow
And the young man
My only son

Our processional led us through
The labyrinth of cancer care
Our hope
All but extinguished

On a bed of sickness
He lay for many months

I am she
Who pleaded
For the LORD to come near
And raise his body to life

I am she
Whom Jesus addressed
With gentle words of care and love
Touched my tears
And held my grief
In the palm of his hands

It is he
My son
Whom Jesus touched
Banishing the chokehold of death
To the astonishment of the crowd

It is he
Whom Jesus raised
To life

It is he
Whom Jesus gave back to me
His mother

It is he
My only son
Who walks in our midst
Healed and whole
To rise to a new day

—Jan Woltmann


A complete regression of a high-grade, inoperable brainstem glioma is basically considered "mission impossible" in the world of medicine.

To say it is rare is generous. To say it's right up there with raising the dead is more like it. Radiation and chemotherapy are stopgap measures to give patients a few extra months or years, at best.

But a complete regression or disappearance? That outcome shatters all categories of medical understanding.

"Diddly," became Schneider's favorite word to describe what he saw on successive MRIs. The tests happened at regular intervals, every three months. We would toss and turn through those weeks, our bodies living on a high wire of anxiety, waiting for results under the fluorescents of a cold clinic room.

Schneider would appear in the doorway, an unkempt vision of eccentric energy, endearingly brilliant, to announce what he saw, which was precisely, in scientific terms, "Diddly!"

Seemingly overnight, we were thrust into a different story. The malignant brain tumor story, according to empirical date, had but one imminent ending. Death.

Even as we prayed with Henry and believed another story was in the making, we were suspended. Probability and possibility waged a tug-of-war within our hearts. Trust, hope, preparation, dread—each took their turn in our psyches.

And the battle continued . . . until the MRI on February 24, announcing the in-breaking of a new narrative.

Today, some seven years later, when I tell this story to someone new, a colleague perhaps, or a neighbor I haven't seen in years, describing Nate's brainstem tumor and its subsequent disappearance, the response is always the same.

"A miracle!" the person will say.

"Yes," I respond.

What follows is usually a slender pause, a stupefied silence, a slipping into wonder. I see it pass over the person's face, if only for a moment. The glossy eyes, the way the mouth curls into a smile, the softening expression, a shiver. This is especially true if the person is a parent. Something always stirs deep within.

That's the effect of a miracle on human consciousness. That's what happens when we are thrown back on our heels by an event that defies all categories of natural or scientific law.

In the end, it can only be explained by the intervention of the divine. That's why the word "miracle" reaches beyond its Latin origins (*miraculum*) to a Greek word found scattered throughout the Gospels—*teras*, simply meaning "a wonder."

"Wonder, that astonished willingness to stop what we are doing, to stand still, open-eyed and open-handed, ready to take in what is *more* and *other*."[1]

---

1. Peterson, *Christ Plays*, 127.

In the days following the MRI report, we slipped into a place of wonder. We stayed there, stupefied, awestruck, mostly in shock.

All we knew was that this miracle, this event that shifted our universe from sick to well, from diseased to healthy, from tumor cloud to its disappearance, left us speechless.

Nate was saved. There were no words for the unsayable, the unexplainable, the irrational, this resurrection. This healing was mysterious. The place we now stood was holy. The best we could do was "bow before the mystery."[2]

"The Lord has done this, and it is marvelous in our eyes," declared my dad, repeating the refrain from Psalm 118:23.

*Yes! Yes! Yes!*

We bowed in our bodies, beside our beds, at the kitchen table, on the living room floor. We bowed in our hearts—again and again in the days following the MRI revelation.

Joy erupted around our dinner table; gratitude spilled over to our people. This story would live its legend in our bones. It would change our family narrative.


When I unspool my imagination, really let it go, I try to imagine how it happened, when those hands of Jesus touched upon Nate's head and released that kingdom-come into his brainstem. Was it during radiation? In the midst of Henry's prayers? While Nate was sleeping?

To "get inside the miracle, to catch him at it,"[3] is out of reason's reach. It belongs to a different realm.

Miracles, in the true sense of the word, invite us to be present to mystery, to be with our wonder, to hand ourselves over and let go of our compulsive need to observe, measure, and analyze. Miracles invite us to free fall into faith with all our faculties, wide-eyed and wide-open to that which is beyond our usual way of knowing.

To birth a child is to be present to mystery; to touch a growing belly and wonder how on earth all those cells know what to do. The womb is a place of mystery. So is the heart.

"Though the human body is born complete in one moment," says John O'Donohue, "the human heart is never completely born. It is being birthed in every experience of your life. Everything that happens to you has the potential to deepen you. It brings to birth within you new territories of the heart."[4]

2. MacNutt, *Healing*, 147.

3. Shaw, *Accompanied by Angels*, 79.

4. O'Donohue, *Anam Cara*, 26.

Miracles are like that. A new life is born complete in one moment: a baby, a blossom, a brainstem. Glory, the "light-filled word," is on full display, "spilling out the extravagant brightness that marks God's presence among us."[5] There is wonder, an unutterable sense of being in the presence of glory.

Yet the heart's work has just begun, stretching into, holding the possibilities of what it means to live, to receive, to trust, to inhabit this new world and breathe its air.

It was an audacious claim to say Nate was healed, perhaps somewhat hasty. I see that now.

There is a miracle—*an event*. And there is healing—*a process*. What we didn't know then was that this event that split our cosmos into *before* and *after*, that resurrected us from death, would take time, months, years, in fact, to live into.

Healing is incremental. Much like the dawn, there is the faintest hint of light in the night sky followed by its increase, until at last, the sun banishes the darkness. A slow and steady rise.

It makes me wonder how those people Jesus healed in the Gospel stories went back into their families, their communities, their synagogues. Everything had changed. Who were they in the after-land, the place of rebirth? How did others see them? How did they see themselves? Would they forever be identified by their illness—the paralyzed man, the blind man, the woman with the blood disorder, the leper, the girl with demons. The Gospels don't say.

Who was blind Bartimaeus after Jesus restored his sight (Mark 10:46–52)? For years, maybe decades, Bartimaeus had begged by the roadside. Suddenly, he found himself squinting into the light as his heart danced into new territories. Yet he was unemployed; he would need to find new rhythms, new skills, a new way to make a living.

And what about the man living in the cemetery (Mark 5:1–20), possessed by demons, bent on self-destruction, cutting his body with rocks? All those neuropathways made new in his encounter with Jesus—new territories of the mind opened up, his demons banished.

Yet, the scars on his body and soul would continue to remind him of his former life. Even in a new season, his parents may have faced interrogation, the religious order may have been outraged, neighbors may have been stuck in the past, children may have fled. He may have suffered from post-traumatic stress disorder.

Did it take time to work out this grace? The Gospels don't say.

---

5. Peterson, *Christ Plays*, 99.

"When we have encountered Christ's healing presence in ways that do not fit existing paradigms," says Ruth Haley Barton, "we might find ourselves on the outside for a while. That's the bad news."[6]

Living with a miracle can be complicated, controversial, maybe even scandalous.

"Party? When's the party?" asked a friend in the hours following the good news. "Really, there must be a party."

Quite right! I wanted to throw something splendid right then. I really did. I imagined the scene in my mind, our house bursting with family and friends, our shining faces reflecting the joy in our hearts.

But the truth was we were utterly exhausted by the intensity of treatment, the weeks of waiting and willing ourselves to stay with the day, and the mountain of uncertainty we traversed in the final week leading up to the results. All these months gathering ourselves around the possibility of death, living in the shadow of Good Friday. It would take time to let this miracle make its way into the creases of our existence, to live as Easter people.

"I don't know how to live out of this new reality," Nate said. "I'm frustrated with myself, I don't feel like celebrating. What's wrong with me?"

"There's no on and off switch," said my wise husband. "Thoughts don't go away overnight."

We opted for a steak dinner with our family to celebrate. I purchased a new sweater for the occasion. How long had it been since we dressed up and ventured out together? I couldn't remember the last time.

Norm and I held hands under the table, reveling in the scene, content to be silent amid the happy banter of our children, blissful witnesses to lighthearted conversation. To anyone around us, we looked ordinary enough. But we carried with us something extraordinary, a secret joy we were still unwrapping.

When the bill arrived at the table, we were shocked to see it was paid in full. Warren stood in the doorway.

The decision to continue chemotherapy was surprisingly controversial. After all, God had healed Nate, right? The MRI had said so. Some in our circle felt that follow-up chemotherapy was unnecessary, maybe even a nod to something missing in our faith.

6. Barton, "The Journey," 81.

Even Henry, who had been fully supportive of every medical intervention to date, said, "God can do the mop-up—why would you subject Nate's body to the brutality of chemotherapy when the tumor has disappeared?"

Still others in our inner circle felt it was the responsible thing to do. "There's still some inflammation in the brainstem," Warren said after combing through the radiologist report.

Ultimately, it was Nate's call to follow through with the plan for chemotherapy. It was his body, his future. Whatever he decided, we would be fully supportive; Nate would not be alone in the process.

The three of us hashed over the possibilities, contemplating what twice the dose of temozolomide might do to his body, just beginning to flourish and revive with energy. The picture was not pretty; the process was anything but easy. But, somehow, it felt completely wrong to bail on the medical community who we believed God had gathered, partnered with, and was working through to accomplish his purposes.

Where was the line between human and divine agency? Who could say? And what if we didn't go through with the chemo and the cancer returned? How would we feel knowing we didn't do everything within our reach to do? Where was the handbook on healing?

In the end, Nate chose to say "yes."

"God will get him through," affirmed Henry.

On February 29, five days after receiving news of the tumor's disappearance, Nate began his first round at double the dose of temozolomide.

For five days, I watched the young man before me lose his color and slowly retreat into the place where chemo does its best work: where mouth sores, nausea, head pain, and extreme fatigue wreak havoc with the body and the mind. The Neupogen, intended to stabilize his blood counts, left Nate with debilitating bone ache, the unlikely side effect mentioned by the CancerCare pharmacist. He went through pain meds like candy.

Sadness followed. Nate was sad he had to deal with a life-threatening disease; sad his friends didn't understand; sad he didn't have the energy to get off the couch; sad he would not return to his summer job. Nate was sad that his future looked so uncertain.

Living with a miracle can be messy.

It may also require a certain kind of silence.


OF THE THIRTY-SEVEN MIRACLES recorded in the Gospels, three involve dying or dead children. They are now among my favorites.

There is Jesus and the Widow of Nain, her dead son brought back to life in the middle of the young man's funeral procession. The story is short, only seven verses in the Gospel of Luke. But it includes one of the most tender scenes recorded in all the miracle narratives.

Commenting on this passage (Luke 7:11–17), Pope Francis says, "The Greek verb that indicates [Jesus'] compassion is *splanchnizomai*, which derives from the word that indicates internal organs or the mother's womb. It is similar to the love of a father and mother who are profoundly moved by their own son; it is a visceral love."[7]

Then, in the Gospel of John (4:43–54), there is the story of the government official's son. The official goes in search of Jesus because his son is dying.

"Go home," Jesus tells him, "your son lives."

The official believes, goes on his way, and discovers that his son had been healed at the very moment Jesus had said the word.

Although more than 2,000 years separate us, I am among these parents. I recognize the desperation in their eyes, the urgency in their petition, their impatience for Jesus to come, to touch, to speak, to revive what is most precious.

There is a third story, though. It appears in three out of four Gospels—Matthew, Mark, and Luke—highlighting the story's importance, telling us we ought to pause, sit up, and pay attention, maybe even be on the watch for something wonderful.

The story is about a twelve-year-old girl who is palliative. The girl's father, Jairus, a religious leader and desperate parent, begs Jesus to come to his home and touch his terminally ill daughter, his only child.

But on the way, Jesus is delayed and Jairus receives the devastating news that his daughter has died.

"Don't be afraid," says Jesus, "just believe."

When they finally arrive, a crowd has gathered. The house is full of mourners, people crying and wailing loudly.

"The girl is not dead, she's asleep," says Jesus. The crowd laughs at him, even mocks him.

At that point, Jesus shoos them out—actually, more like *drives* them out. Maybe he says something like, "Beat it, scram!"

Alone in the room with three of his disciples and the parents, Jesus takes the girl by the hand and says, "Little girl, get up." And she does, much to the astonishment of that little band of five. Her parents slip into a place of wonder.

But here's the bewildering part: Jesus tells the parents to keep quiet.

"Don't tell a soul what happened in this room," he instructs.

---

7. Pope Francis, *The Name of God*, 92.

I always thought this was odd. Why? Why would Jesus say such a thing? Yet, in the aftermath of our own experience, I hear this story differently.

How long had the parents lived with this child's illness, standing in the shadow of Good Friday with their only child, their hearts demolished more each day by her slow decline? The Gospels don't say.

But here is what I imagine: Long after the crowds scatter, and the chatter and gossip of the miracle recedes, the family is around the dinner table with their beloveds in the lamplight—wonder still on their faces, their joy spilling out in every direction. The story lives its legend in their bones. It will change their family narrative; it will resurrect their future.

And maybe what they need most for this grace to do its work is *time*—months, even years. Maybe they need to *live* the mystery instead of *explain* it to the crowds. Maybe this is their pathway to healing. Maybe Jesus knows this.

Wherever there are people who have lost their sense of wonder, people who are more interested in gathering facts than listening with their hearts, there are crowds. They exist in the neighborhood, marketplace, and workplace, in families and even churches.

There were crowds in our story, too. People who had not traveled closely with us, others who remained at a distance. Still, they had heard rumors of Nate's story. They had questions and curiosities, doubts and skepticism not easily addressed in short exchanges. Always, these interactions hijacked my peace and held me hostage to our perceived place of peril.

"What do the doctor's say? Why is Nate still on chemotherapy? Is this some sort of remission?"

"Well, no, not really; we believe it's a miracle," I would reply, sometimes in a tone so timid I felt it betrayed my belief. The words felt strange on my tongue. I doubt I was ready to say them out loud.

How could one explain being caught by such an unexpected mercy when others were not? Maybe mercy is messy. Maybe mercy, in that season, was to be cupped over, held gently.

To rehearse the facts, to explain any meaningful part of the story, to defend its mystery diminished its enormity and depleted my energy. Inevitably, I would walk away from such compressed conversations in a grocery store, or at some kind of gathering, either angry at myself for saying anything or angry at the other person for their apparent lack of sensitivity.

Inevitably, something got ripped away on the inside.

The wound was tender. The story was a precious pearl best shared in the company of the committed, around a dinner table, on familiar couches, in front of a fire. This story was a mystery best savored in the lamplight of our liminal community, told and retold with care, in ways hushed, holy, and unhurried.

Maybe that's why Jesus uttered those bewildering words: "Don't tell a soul what happened in this room."

"Words often leave us with a sense of inner defeat," writes Henri Nouwen. "They can even create a sense of numbness and a feeling of being bogged down in swampy ground. Often they leave us in a slight depression, or in a fog that clouds the window of our mind."[8]

A fifth-century Church Father once said, "When the door of the steam bath is continually left open, the heat inside rapidly escapes through it; likewise the soul, in its desire to say many things, dissipates its remembrance of God through the door of speech, even though everything it says may be good. . . . Timely silence, then, is precious, for it is nothing less than the mother of the wisest thoughts."[9]

"To try to talk about the unsayable to the crowds," says Richard Rohr, "is to trivialize it, or even to lose its depth, like describing great lovemaking to an outsider."[10]

Miracles may invite us to stillness and silence. They may ask us to hold onto mercy in the company of a few trusted souls, to believe that the One who spoke a word of healing over us will bring it to fullness.

Miracles may invite us to walk into a new reality and let it claim us, inch by inch, until we can live into its dimensions, inhabit it as home.


The first round of chemotherapy did not go well. There were setbacks. In week four, when Nate should have started his second round of chemo, he came down with a nasty flu virus. In week five, his blood counts were still well below the acceptable levels, even with Neupogen. Nate was again frustrated by the apparent weakness of his own body.

Then came the news of my dad.

My dad had been hospitalized in January for a week due to kidney pain. Tests were done. Time passed. Dad was referred to a specialist in Regina in early February, a city two hours away from his home, where more tests were done, and more information gathered.

By mid-March, doctors had determined that the kidney pain stemmed from an aggressive form of blood cancer—multiple myeloma. Chemotherapy was immediate.

8. Nouwen, *The Way of the Heart*, 52.

9. Diadochus of Photiki, "On Spiritual Knowledge," 276.

10. Rohr, *The Naked Now*, 119–120.

In mid-April, my dad and Nate both began their second round of chemotherapy. My dad was seventy-nine, my son was twenty-one. The oldest
and youngest on my side of the family, together in treatment.

Coaching my dad on the best anti-nausea medication and how to eat
a diet rich in protein was beyond ironic. It was an absurdity. What's more,
I couldn't jump in my car and drive the nine hours to their home, like I did
when my mom was diagnosed with cancer some six years earlier.

Back then, it had been easy. Despite my dad's protests, his stoic
insistence that they were doing "just fine," I had packed my bags and
showed up on their doorstep to see my mom incapacitated on the couch,
her usual chatter silenced by relentless rounds of radiation. They had not
been fine at all.

The same was true now. I heard it in my mom's voice. I ached to be
close.

# 15

## Mice Droppings

Some inner urgency was rising, some energy gusting through our souls, guiding our search. God, is that you?

—Jan Woltmann

By early May, we were searching for reprieve, somewhere, anywhere that wasn't this place, these four walls, and this relentless rhythm.

The CancerCare calendar which determined our days provided a small opening at the end of the second round, a four-day break—away from pills, needles, bloodwork, and homecare workers; away from the pressing reality of an upcoming MRI. Had it already been three months?

The first week of May was early to stay at the family-owned cottage, a sixty-minute drive north of the city. We usually saved the official opening for the May long weekend. Nevertheless, we latched on to the idea of going out there like a life preserver, receiving permission and a list of instructions from Norm's dad: Watch for leaks in the waterline. Check the pilot light on the furnace. Open the flue in the fireplace.

It didn't matter that it might take a few hours to settle in. This space allowed us to change our geography, to drive past the Perimeter Highway until the forest swallowed up the roadway, to inhale air scented with earth and pine, to smell new life in this patch of planet under the spell of the springtime sun.

The family cottage had always been our place of respite. Maybe it could help us forget, even for a few days, about our precarious circumstances; about my dad; about cancer and chemotherapy; about a disease that demanded every shred of human energy. Maybe it could help us remember the miracle in our midst and hold it tight. Our hopes were high.

It was also our twenty-seventh wedding anniversary. Other years, we celebrated by driving west to the Rocky Mountains of Banff, our honeymoon destination. With the accounting busy season behind him, Norm could finally relax and we could find each other again. Not this year.

We arrived with our small suitcases and bags of groceries crammed in the truck box of Norm's Ridgeline, with Ruby curled close on Nate's lap. It was the puppy's first road trip. The day was unusually chilly and gray; the cottage cold and musty. No matter. Nothing that a warm fire couldn't fix. We got down to the work of unpacking.

But wait! *What are those?*

We found some in the cupboard under the sink. Then, upon closer inspection, more on the kitchen floor, in the drawer that held the pots and pans, beneath the sofa cushions. Mice droppings! We were completely unprepared for this hazard of cabin-opening. It was everywhere.

"We'll vacuum the floors and disinfect the counters," I said defiantly to Norm, who was fiddling with the fireplace. Meanwhile, Nate was trying to contain a very excited Ruby on the front porch of the cottage. The whole scene was clearly making him anxious and overwhelmed.

"Nate, why don't you go upstairs and lie down while we figure this out," I urged, in a tone that came out high-pitched and forced.

I tried to contain my panic, to stay calm while my mind raced with catastrophes. Nate's body was compromised by chemo. Mice droppings potentially carried hantavirus—a virus that becomes airborne when cleaning up the remains.

"Something's wrong," I screeched to Norm in my haste to vacuum. "There's no power— there's no suction. It's broken!"

I went upstairs to find Nate, to check in. He was lying on the bed.

"We can't even enjoy a couple of days away," he whimpered through frustrated tears.

And that's when I noticed them. Stray droppings, maybe just three, that lay beyond the pillow on the exposed white sheet.

My heart sank. This was not a safe place to spend the next few days.

The drive home was quiet. There was no making this better. Anger, disappointment, and sadness swirled around the cab of our truck like so many black flies. Swatting them away proved useless.

But the experience triggered something for me and Norm. Maybe because we felt defeated, out of control, at the mercy of mice droppings; or maybe because, at a cellular level, we knew that whatever dreams we had or were putting off for "someday" were well worth examining in the now.

Cancer brings clarity to time, to relationships, to savings. The idea began at the edge of our imagination, when our bitter complaints and self-pity were wrung out. Soon enough, it would become fully formed, lodging itself in our hearts, changing the landscape and texture of our lives for years to come.

At first we called it a diversion. Later, we called it a leading, this desire to find a place of our own, an address off the grid and in the woods.

A WEEK AFTER THE family cottage debacle, on May 11, Nate was scheduled for an MRI. Mercifully, the MRI and the read would take place on the same day. We would not wait five days for results. We had no reason to believe anything had changed. Yet our bodies, especially Nate's, held enough trauma from a time six months earlier when everything had. Time and grace would eventually diminish, but never eliminate, the kind of anxiety that came at us in three-month intervals.

I phoned Henry to come and pray with us the night before the MRI. It would be the last time we would see him. After a year in Winnipeg, and a week of fasting, he and his wife discerned it was time to move east, to a place in Quebec where French-speaking Pentecostal pastors were needed.

Henry showed up with a bright smile and warm embrace. When it came time to pray, he stood over Nate and placed his right hand on his head in a stance that had become so familiar to us over these months. This voice that had thundered through the darkness of our darkest hour in November, that had petitioned the presence of Jesus with passionate fervor in the days leading up to the miracle MRI and had announced God's word of healing the night before, now began to sing softly in hushed tones.

"Thank you, thank you, thank you." He began in English to a tune that sounded like it had come from the heart of his African homeland. Then came a language I did not know, a Nigerian dialect maybe, a strange tongue. Gone were the fire and energy of intercession, and in their place a kind of lullaby, soothing, peaceful, piercing the fear in our hearts.

For Henry, it was finished, the travail, the fasting, the work of prayer. All that was left was thanksgiving, offered with humility, from a guttural place. In my lifetime, I doubt I will ever hear a melody so beautiful, so soulful, so unequivocally comforting. His song would stay with me and sing itself back to my heart at three-month intervals.

We said our goodbyes to Henry with hugs and tears. This man who had been both priest and prophet to us, who had answered the call to come.

"Who will pray with us now?" said Nate, his face stricken.

The next day, we trudged to CancerCare and braced ourselves for the MRI results.

"Diddly," announced Schneider.

We could hear it on the inside, the echo of Henry's song.

MEANWHILE, THE COTTAGE BANTER—THE possibility of buying a modest property—escalated in earnest. We drew lines around our criteria: location, price, proximity to the city.

The area surrounding Winnipeg is cabin country. During the summer months, the city experiences an exodus—people vacate the city in droves for lake life in all directions. To the east, ninety minutes away, is the Canadian Shield, imposing rocks, boreal forests, and winding roads, pocked by deep, cold lakes. To the north is Lake Winnipeg, one of the world's largest freshwater lakes, all sand and shoreline for miles.

Most of our friends owned cottages to the east in the Shield. In previous years, we flirted with breaking from our roots to the north and buying there, foregoing sand and shore for rock and dock.

But deep in these circumstances, we sifted our desires. Because of the back-and-forth nature of hospital visits for the foreseeable future, we needed to be close to the city, no more than an hour away. Now, more than ever, it was more important to be in the vicinity of the family cottage and the memories that shaped our history.

This was our land. These were our people.

Everything for sale within a five-mile radius came up short: too small, too expensive, or too old—we had neither the skills nor energy for a fixer-upper.

"What about this one?" said Norm one evening, scrolling on his tablet.

I came over and planted myself on the couch beside him. If nothing else, this little cottage-buying adventure provided some interior lift, a bit of oxygen for our spirits after plunging headlong into round three of chemotherapy treatment with Nate.

Although I couldn't put my finger on the feeling, it did remind me of our decision back in November involving a certain little canine companion. A gear on the inside suddenly shifted. Some inner urgency was rising, some energy gusting through our souls, guiding our search. *God, is that you?*

It's hard to explain this sense of guidance, interior wisdom, God in the middle of things—God within the crisis. "Words, like yes, no, this not that, now, not yet, are part of it, but it doesn't come in words, nor even thoughts," says Gerald May. "It's more like an energy in a certain direction when the time is right for something, and a fatigue in that direction when it's not."[1]

*Yes, that's it.* Without knowing it, we had been living this way since Nate's diagnosis, attentive, present with all our senses and instincts to the needs of any given moment. Gone was any shred of care for living in half-measures, of doing what life expected. We began each day with deep gratitude and prayed for Holy Spirit-help to get through it. Mostly, it felt like living wide-awake, fully alert, every plan subjected to the now of our life-energy. Without the usual constraints, without those attitudes and perceptions that had slowly tamed us over time, we were fearless, even wild.

"A brand-new A-frame?" I asked. "On the water? Where exactly?"

"According to this map, it's located right here, on this stretch of shoreline," said Norm, his index finger tracing the slim line that doglegged off the familiar highway.

"Can you believe it?" he said. "All these years, we've been driving right past this place. Who knew there were cottages, dozens of them, whole developments along this part of the lake?"

"It's out of our price range," I said quickly, cautiously, in a tone that begged to be challenged.

"No harm in looking," said Norm with a wink.

We called the realtor and arranged to see the cottage the following Sunday, May 20.

---

1. May, *The Wisdom of Wilderness*, 45.

# 16

## The Healing Place

**THE PEACE OF WILD THINGS**

When despair for the world grows in me
and I wake in the night at the least sound
in fear of what my life and my children's lives may be,
I go and lie down where the wood drake
rests in his beauty on the water, and the great heron feeds.
I come into the peace of wild things
who do not tax their lives with forethought
of grief. I come into the presence of still water.
And I feel above me the day-blind stars
waiting with their light. For a time
I rest in the grace of the world, and am free.

—WENDELL BERRY[1]

DURING THE BLEAK MONTHS of uncertainty, in the death-grip of cancer, there was a picture taped to our fridge, a guiding image. I would call it an icon. It came to us as an e-mail attachment, part of an encouraging note from my uncle in California.

1. Berry, *The Selected Poems*, 30.

"He will cover you with his feathers, and under his wings you will find refuge," he wrote, quoting Psalm 91:4. I doubt he knew the impact the verse and image would have; that we would eventually frame them, positioning them as the focal point of our home.

The picture featured a close-up of a green pigeon, perched on a tree branch, her mama-eyes wide open, on the watch. On either side, tucked in close, were her chicks, barely visible, covered by her massive wings. A quick glance and one could easily overlook those little creatures, safely nestled in their mother's warmth.

This was an image of God, fully feminine, and it took hold of my imagination. Mighty maternal feathers covering us with grace, enough for the day, sheltering us with fierce compassion, looking out for our good.

Regardless of how bad our circumstances were, I gazed at those chicks and prayed for the grace to see myself there—hidden under her expansive and wild wingspan.

Saturday finally arrived. It was an overcast morning, the air warmed with humidity, smelling of new earth, fresh with possibility. We picked up coffees, Norm and I, and slipped out of the city, just the two of us.

It felt sublime and strangely surreal. We rehearsed all the positives of this purchase like a pair of teenagers, adrenaline pumping, excitement spilling. "The place is perfect," we cooed.

True, the price was more—a lot more—than we wanted to pay. But we had worked the numbers and, together, agreed on an amount, lower than the asking. Maybe it was a long shot, maybe we were dreaming, but we had a feeling, a strong surge in our core.

Thirty minutes into the drive, the busy four-lane highway narrowed into a two-lane, ushering us into the familiar and welcoming tree-lined sanctuary. Spring 2012 was unusually warm, in the high teens during the months of March and April. Lush green carpeted the ditches and the fields and completely covered the poplars, their leaves shivering and shiny on this misty morning.

There was a steady stream of cars for a Saturday, signaling a change of season, an entire community of cottagers awakening from winter slumber. No doubt, others like us were looking at a property for the first time, responding to something primal that beckoned this time of year.

"It's your next left," I said to Norm, as cars whizzed past us in the opposite direction. This stretch of two-lane always made me nervous. "Why are people in such a hurry?" I muttered, "Isn't the whole point of escaping the city to slow down?"

Once on the side road, away from the fray of traffic, our speed slowed, and our shoulders slid down a few inches. Norm popped the Ridgeline's sunroof and suddenly the little space was full of bird sounds and fresh air.

We followed the dogleg onto the gravel road that ran parallel to the lake. We passed lakeside developments with breezy summer names, one after the other—Sandy Shores, Island Estates, Pine Bay. We turned into Sunset Cove.

"Just fifty minutes from our door," I said, checking the time. *Unbelievable.*

The "For Sale" sign hung haphazardly in the ditch beside the driveway. It was all but hidden in the tall grass surrounding it. How long had it been on the market? The price, the location on the lake—why hadn't anyone snatched up this piece of paradise? *God, could this be true?*

The sound of the truck doors slamming reverberated through the silence. The air was a medley of the earth's fragrance—pine, sand, and shore on this humid afternoon in mid-May.

It was magical how the forest surrounding the property ignited my senses, possessing a kind of enchantment all its own. How tall were those white pines, standing like sentinels off to the side, their tips swaying slightly in the southern breeze? *Spectacular.*

How ironic that the 1,500 square-foot A-frame was a Health Science Centre lottery prize cottage just a year before our world was rocked by Nate's deadly diagnosis and regular visits to CancerCare at that very hospital. Coincidence? No. Life was too full of miracles, big and small, to believe that. Somehow this cottage was made to measure, right-sized just for us.

According to our real estate agent, Larry, and his eighty-year-old dad and business partner, Chuck, the lucky lottery winners were a young couple from a large subdivision on the north side of the city. They had neither the means to maintain the place, nor the desire. They were campers not cottagers, so they put the cottage on the market shortly after in hopes of getting something close to its estimated worth.

"Hello," said Larry, greeting us pleasantly. "Did you have trouble finding the place?"

"No," said Norm, all smiles. "I've passed this place every summer for most of my life and never knew it existed."

Once in the door, we were ushered into the great room, vaulted and wide-open, a kitchen-dining-living area under a ceiling of tongue and groove pine beams that smelled of fresh varnish. It was intoxicating.

The elder, Chuck, made himself at home on the sleek brown leather couch facing the black granite fireplace framed in chunky pine. Larry found a chair at the round dining table, a front row seat to . . . what exactly?

The floor-to-ceiling windows were meant to showcase Lake Winnipeg, but the ocean-like body of water was barely visible, a forest of towering birch and ash trees obstructing the view. Every other patch of the frontage was thick and lush with poplar and evergreen shoots, so much so that I gasped. Yes, it was completely overgrown in its jungle appearance, but there was something else. What exactly?

Intuitively, I moved closer to the window. And then I knew before my reason registered: It was a canopy, a covering, an expansive and wild wingspan.

"Sunsets every night," said Chuck.

"Sensational sunsets," said Larry with a cheesy grin.

I almost laughed out loud. Yes, the two of them were quite the sales team. How could either of them possibly know how the sunsets looked with all those trees and that carpet of underbrush?

"What do you think?" I whispered to Norm.

"Amazing!" he said. "It looks and smells brand new."

"It's true," I said, as I scanned the ebony kitchen cabinets and the black granite countertops that contrasted so beautifully with the wide-plank flooring. I imagined the smoothness of the countertops under my fingertips. A grand staircase led to the master bedroom, with its fully equipped ensuite bathroom and walk-in closet.

This was clearly more luxury-lake-house and less quaint-cottage, something Larry was quick to point out. It boasted the best of made-in-Manitoba materials and craftsmanship.

All the bedrooms were tastefully furnished and lavishly accented with rustic linens and throw pillows. There were granite countertops in both bathrooms and tall, rectangular statement mirrors propped behind the oval sinks. A massive pair of weathered boat oars, the kind that belonged to a bygone era, provided a focal point on the vaulted wall in the great room, and part of a moose antler hung above the fireplace. Paintings of poplar trees and shorelines were tastefully mounted throughout, their hues harmonizing with the world beyond the windows. It was the work of a skilled decorator, a page out of my favorite designer magazine. *Dreamy.*

Was I smitten? Absolutely, it was hard not to be.

"It appears the cottage is unfinished," said Norm, when the lively banter with Larry turned serious. "No deck, no landscaping, no shed."

After almost three decades married to the man, I knew this tone of voice. My husband was beginning to negotiate. There would be much more to discuss on the drive home.

"But you can't deny that every other detail is done to perfection," said Larry.

"There's a major crack in the wall in the kitchen," I said.

"Just normal shifting of the house," Larry said.

"And the molding above that moon window in the master bedroom," I said, "it's completely unfinished at the top."

"Good eye," he said, indulging my doubts with a wink.

The conversation went back and forth for the next half hour. At every opportunity, the two realtors gushed about the development, how close it was to the new harbor for boat owners, how renowned the area was for pickerel and ice fishing, how the vegetation was so diverse.

"And don't forget the beach," said Larry. "The cottage is less than ten minutes away from Grand Beach, the finest beach in Manitoba, if not all of Canada."

THE POSSESSION DATE WAS June 27, 2012, the date of Nate's twenty-second birthday. Coincidence? No.

In our wildest dreams, we couldn't have imagined this day six months earlier, or even a month ago at the mice-infested family cottage.

We celebrated Nate's birthday in fine style that year, the family gathered at the lake house for the two-day festivities. Fireworks lit up the night sky while fireflies danced in the front yard. Around that time, we discovered that our oldest daughter was pregnant with our first grandchild. God was full of surprises, showing off it seemed.

We stood on the threshold of this new place, fully aware that we were people living under gift, recipients of radical grace, *solo gratia*.

True, Nate was still extremely sick, experiencing the dreadful side effects of chemotherapy, now in the middle of his third round, the halfway mark of treatment. Yet something was changing, the scenery all around us and within us told us so. New energy was returning to our weary bodies and hope was throbbing through our broken hearts.

This cottage, nestled in green foliage, warmed by the summer sun was pure provision. This was our place of refuge, as if we were being taken into God's self, taken under the sheltering Presence.

The earth was bursting with hospitality, full of soul. Majestic birds welcomed us to the land: pileated woodpeckers knocked on the trees, bald eagles crisscrossed overhead and nested nearby, osprey dove for fish on the sandbank. Black-caped chickadees greeted us each morning and throughout the day with their delicate song, bright notes from beyond, coming through the open windows in surround sound.

All seemed to be holy messengers. All seemed to have been sent to us that summer, winged creatures, agents of grace, participating in our healing.

"Look and listen for God in creation," said the ancient Celts of Iona. "The ladder that connects heaven and earth is everywhere present."[2]

As if that weren't enough, just beyond the jungle brush of our windowed haven, beyond the bank overgrown with wild grasses and clover, was a watery horizon, so vast that it seemed to us an ocean.

During the day, when the sun was high and the sky and cloud shimmered their dazzling blue on the water, we caught a glimpse of something beyond the chemo cycles. The horizon spoke to us of a future, it whispered hope in its never-ending beauty, water and sky, a merging eternity, hinting at more, always more, like a curtain pulled back, a veil.

And when the full-orbed sun, flickering shades of magenta and tangerine on the glassy water, slowly disappeared into its northern edge at dusk, we witnessed the glory of our story, the miracle, gathered up in the greater story, an ancient story, all held in the mystery of the sun and its seasons. We were hidden under a great and mighty wingspan.

"Surely goodness and mercy shall follow me all the days of my life," says the ancient psalm. The verb in this verse, "to follow," is a powerful, active verb, suggesting pursuit—God's friendliness and kindness running after us, chasing us down, grabbing us and holding us tight.[3]

"Our life is not willed by God to be an endless anxiety," says Old Testament theologian Walter Brueggemann, "it is rather meant to be an embrace, but that entails being caught by God."[4] We felt caught all right, in the best way.

And if the birds and the horizon weren't enough, the presence of the monarchs should have tipped us off to God's gracious generosity, his kindness wrapped around us. A milder winter, an earlier spring, maybe favorable winds, meant that Manitoba witnessed one of the largest migrations of monarch butterflies that summer. They were everywhere, thousands of them, flitting around our feet as we walked through the grass, flying beside us as we drove, hovering over us as we sat on the shoreline.

This was the same creature with the unflinching gaze that had landed on Norm's finger the previous summer, fanning its wings and promising us Presence before our descent into darkness. This little creature, our holy messenger of hope, now met us at every turn.

To be claimed, to be caught, to be taken in, this is the mercy measured in inches, feet, and miles in the geography that surrounds us. This is the

---

2. Newell, *Listening*, 89.

3. Brueggemann, *A Way*," 32.

4. Brueggemann, *A Way*, 32.

mercy of *place*, where the "presence of God is vibrantly incarnate, palpable, alive, and accessible to our own hands and feet."[5]

God's presence is in the land, pulsing under foot and in the particularities of our surroundings: birch and ash trees, white pines and clover, black-caped chickadees, lapping waves, setting sun.

In summer 2012, the land we were given addressed us, called our names, invited us to sit awhile on her shores and allow her created goodness to do its work of healing. To my ears, it sounded like the refrain from the old doxology I sang in four-part harmony when I was a child, the one I still pray from the Book of Hours: *Praise God, from whom all blessings flow; Praise him, all creatures here below; Praise him above, you heavenly host; Praise Father, Son and Holy Ghost.*[6]

I would hear the same song some years later on the shores of Iona. Celtic spirituality, part of an ancient stream of contemplative spirituality, perceived these doxological rhythms in the elements of creation.

"Recognize the world as a place of revelation and the whole of life as sacramental,"[7] said the Celts. This ancient people understood that life with the Trinity was life with the land, that the spiritual and material are inextricably linked, knit together with mystery.

WE WERE HOME HERE in a way we had never experienced before. It would claim us, inch by inch, and heal us over time. It didn't matter that Norm spent most of that summer chopping down trees and clearing bush in an effort to see more water and sky. It didn't matter that most of our retirement savings went toward the purchase. It didn't matter that gas prices skyrocketed that summer, or how often we drove the fifty minutes from our city home to the cottage.

What mattered most was the miracle of life lived each day, together, under the wingspan of wild things.

---

5. Silf, *Inheriting Paradise*, iv.

6. Tickle, *The Divine Hours*, 186.

7. Newell, *Listening*, 3.

# 17

## Finish Line

God knows I am no good at it, but I keep trying, and once or twice I have been lucky, graced. I have been conscious but not conscious of anything, not even of myself . . . I have sensed the presence of a presence. I have felt a promise promised.

—FREDERICK BUECHNER[1]

LIFE BEYOND CHEMOTHERAPY CYCLES, loosed from the world of CancerCare? How would that feel? As freeing as it sounded, it was also terrifying.

We had developed a love-hate relationship with this place that had dictated our rhythms over the past nine months. There was a strange attachment to weekly blood checks and oncologist appointments, an odd assurance that all was well.

Loosed from these structures, we would be on our own to navigate healing. Should Nate begin alternative therapies, like acupuncture, to restore his beat-up immune system? What about plant-based medicines? And fish oil? And what about sugar? Should Nate embrace a radical diet, whole foods only? A plethora of websites said so.

As for Nate, he spoke cautiously about resuming university, or finding work when he was well enough. These type of thoughts propelled Nate forward.

1. Buechner, *Telling Secrets*, 105.

If the chemotherapy rounds went as planned—no delays because of low blood counts or desperately low spirits, the kind that compelled me to ask for an extra week off after Nate's fourth round to muster his body, his emotions, and his will to swallow pills and receive injections—the sixth and final treatment would begin mid-September. Nate would be done by mid-October.

It felt like a lifetime away.

*Thanksgiving is going to be some kind of celebration this year*, I mused dreamily.

But this was mid-August, and there was just one problem.

I looked at the computer-generated letter on the kitchen table and marveled at the clockwork of the CancerCare system; MRIs at three-month intervals were unrelenting. Unlike our experience two weeks ago, where the MRI and the appointment had both mercifully occurred on the same day, this letter indicated we would wait ten days to hear the results of the next MRI. It was an excruciatingly long time for life to be suspended in the ether of unknowing.

Ten days seemed unrealistic; surely the computer had made a mistake. Dr. Schneider would see to the change. I called his office and spoke to his nurse about the dilemma, casually mentioning that Nate's last round of chemo would be over by the October-scheduled MRI.

"There's no such plan," she said, surprised by my comment.

"What?" I asked, "Wait—what do you mean?"

"Nate will continue chemotherapy through fall and into winter," she said matter-of-factly. "Patients like Nate are typically on treatment for a full twelve months."

Silence.

I was stunned. I had no capacity to hear anything more. I stammered and muttered something about Dr. Schneider's words back in February, after news of the miracle MRI, about how Nate would be given six rounds to sweep up any residual rogue cells. To my knowledge, nothing had ever been uttered about *more* treatments, let alone twelve.

"Another six months in temozolomide hell!" cried Nate when he heard the news, his face awash in tears, his body shaking with sobs. "I won't last. I can't do it."

Over the next forty-eight hours I pleaded, we pleaded. *Please God, please show us the way, help us know what to do, which way to turn. Just please make it clear.*

"We are in need of much wisdom and discernment," I wrote to our community in an e-mail a few days before our scheduled meeting with Dr. Schneider on August 24 to discuss the issue.

"With our *whole* heart, we pray that our doctor would sanction a 'release' from this treatment so Nate can have some reprieve from the physical and emotional pain he experiences. At the same time, we desire to be responsible with the information presented. Ultimately, Nate will make the decision. But we desire a blessing of sorts from the medical community in whose care we have been, whose direction we have trusted."

And God answered, in a way that was clear, quiet, and resounding. Not a voice exactly, although the words, and what they meant to me, landed with enough impact that it may as well have been God whispering in my ear.

It was a clear August day at the cottage. The north wind was crashing waves onto the shore in melodic rhythms. It was gloriously soothing to be away from the clamor, to open the *Divine Hours: Prayers for Summertime* to the midday office.

And there it was, all but hidden in the middle of the other readings, a few obscure Old Testament verses from the book of Ecclesiastes, words that at any other time in life I would have skimmed past.

"I know that whatever God does will be forever. To this there is nothing to add, from this there is nothing to subtract" (Ecclesiastes 3:14, NJB).[2]

Of all the verses in the volume of 647 pages, I could not believe that these words appeared on this day. I recognized them alright; they were the words Henry had spoken to us back in April after Nate had completed his first round of chemotherapy.

In April, our family had hosted Henry, his wife, and two daughters for a dinner to say thank you to this man who had been both priest and prophet, who had answered the call to come. It's true that my famous sweet-and-sour meatballs were not an all-time favorite for our African guests. It's also true that Henry and his family weren't very comfortable with the clumsy cutlery. But it didn't matter; we enjoyed each other's company and shared stories.

It was Henry's opinion that Nate did not need to be on chemotherapy, that God could do the mop-up. He had in mind to speak some strong words to us that evening, a sermon about faith and how we should trust God for Nate's healing. But he chose not to when he heard our resolve to stay with the program for the prescribed six cycles. Instead, he gave us two verses from Ecclesiastes, the same verses that were now on the page in front of me.

"I know that whatever God does will be forever. To this there is nothing to add, from this there is nothing to subtract."

I received it as the holy and inspired word that it was—permission. Permission for my mother-heart to let go, permission for Nate to stop

---

2. Tickle, *Prayers for Summertime*, 414.

chemotherapy, permission to trust that the healing in Nate's brainstem was God's work, and that it was good and lasting. Period.

*Thank you,* I whispered into the wind and waves.

The meeting with Dr. Schneider followed. He listened intently to Nate's plea to go off chemo, about my son's experience of feeling battered in body and mind and at his breaking point. Dr. Schneider did not counter with arguments in favor of persisting, nor did he power-up with any form of professional authority that would have elicited a level of guilt and shame for going against his wishes.

No, that wasn't Schneider's way. Instead, he gently explained that his team was not at all sure what they were dealing with when it came to Nate's case. "No one can tell you what will happen," he said to Nate. "There is no medical precedent for your case. Ultimately, this is your decision."

Nate heaved a sigh of relief, as did Norm and I. Here was a man who could admit that he didn't know, who came with a posture of humility to offer his best observations. In the end, when he got up to leave, one hand on the doorknob, he swung around, looked directly at Nate and said with conviction, "No second guessing."

We smiled. *No second guessing.* It was the blessing we needed.


ON THE MORNING OF my forty-ninth birthday, August 30, Nate took me for a drive in his Mazda3, just beyond the Perimeter Highway. Driving his car, grocery shopping with me, texting with friends—all were part of his strategy to celebrate "small wins." It was such a good feeling to be in the passenger seat again.

I remembered where I was a year earlier. A family picture taken at my favorite restaurant in the countryside flashed in my memory—Norm and I with strained smiles, Nate putting on his brave face three weeks after brain surgery, wearing his purple Fanta T-shirt, his head shaved, the incision above his left eye still pink and stitch-marked, his right eye straying off to the side, leaning in with his siblings for a smile. We were battle-worn then, not a clue that the coming months would vault us into some of the worst months of our lives.

Now, a year later, Nate was still here. And despite feeling sick and depressed, he was determined to make this day special for me. We traveled the winding, tree-lined road that led back to the city. Nate was overjoyed by the sight of a cart at the edge of a driveway, boasting a five-gallon white pail bursting with fresh-picked gladiolas. The handmade sign crudely attached to the pail read "Two dollars each."

Gladiolas were my favorite summer flower; during my childhood, they had always bloomed in my grandma's garden on my birthday. It had been my habit on birthday mornings to drive myself to this very spot and choose a bouquet to place in my grandma's vintage vase.

With great pleasure, Nate pulled out some change and placed it in the yogurt container beside the pail. The local grower was evidently not doing this for the money and clearly trusted her customers.

I proudly took my treasures, a stem of variegated orange posies, along with another that bloomed white. That simple, yet beautiful outing still ranks as the best of birthday memories.

"There's no way I can take all these," Nate moaned when he saw the little vial filled to the brim with temozolomide tablets.

Nate's final round of chemotherapy began on September 12—five consecutive days of chemotherapy followed by ten Neupogen injections every other day until October 8.

Small things morphed into full-blown catastrophes, like the pharmacy not receiving the chemotherapy order for the last round. I made a panicked call to the CancerCare pharmacist who took care of it promptly, saying it would be ready the next evening for pickup. Still, I wondered how we would proceed if we didn't receive them on time. Everything ran like clockwork for this program; if chemotherapy was delayed, blood counts could plummet.

Then, when I did pick up the prescription, the denomination of pills had changed. Instead of two pills of temozolomide at 175 milligrams each to be taken first thing in the morning for five days, we were given seven pills at 50 milligrams each. Seven pills first thing, and "only with water," cautioned the pharmacist.

I blanched. Pill-taking was a struggle for Nate at the best of times, especially on days four and five of the cycle. By then, his body would resist the stuff with enough nausea to deter the strongest stomach.

Fortunately, Warren happened to visit, and advised Nate to take the pills with juice or vitamin water to make them more palatable. Nurse Kelly at CancerCare approved the idea. Disaster averted.

Nate's mantra: Just finish!

"Congratulations on getting to the last leg of a very difficult journey," wrote my dad, who was also beginning another round of chemotherapy in Regina. "You will make it the rest of the way, I am convinced."

My dad shared his musings about Jacob, the Old Testament character who wrestled with God for a blessing, the one who, in a dream, saw a staircase to heaven and marked the spot so he would always know where to meet God.

"Jacob was wrong to think that a specific place was key to meeting God," my dad said. "God was always with him. Nate, you and I are always under God's watchful eye. Even when bad things happen, God is there and his angels are there to minister to us."

Something about that e-mail stayed with me. A premonition maybe, a final blessing. I couldn't put my finger on it then.

ON MONDAY EVENING, OCTOBER 15, Nate had his fourth MRI of 2012. The read was scheduled for Friday afternoon, October 19. At least we would hear the results the same week—better than the ten-day spread originally planned.

Ask anyone who waits for results and they will tell you about their anxieties and coping strategies.

We had developed a few of our own for living through the three-month intervals. In response to the unwelcome thoughts that came with a vengeance during the waiting week—the doubts, the what ifs, the dread—we rehearsed Nate's story: the word *Gotcha*, the butterfly, the vision, the dream, the appearance of Henry, the miracle MRI. We reminded each other of all the divinely orchestrated details. We still do.

There were less inspired practices, too, but no less important, at least for me. Like cleaning the house top to bottom and finishing *all* the laundry, even the smelly kitchen towels at the bottom of the heap. My house needed to stay orderly because my emotional world was anything *but*.

It was funny to notice the shelf-life dates on the milk and produce in my grocery cart and think, "By then, we'll know." I planned nothing on my calendar beyond the date of the MRI results. My schedule moved like a planet around these tests.

"There's nothing abnormal in your brainstem," Dr. Schneider announced when he entered the clinic room that Friday. "I scoured the image with three neurosurgeons and we couldn't find a thing."

"Diddly!"

I'll never forget the day, a few months later, when he brought photocopies into the clinic room as evidence. "Before and after pictures," he said, describing the screenshotted images of what he had witnessed on his sophisticated software earlier that morning.

"This is what it looked like back in November 2011," he said, pointing to the big white mass, the dreadful tumor cloud at the base of Nate's skull, a deadly blotch on an otherwise symmetrical background of black and grey brain tissue.

"This is what it looks like now," he said, wearing his astonishment and waving the clear picture in front of Nate. "It's completely gone!"

"Wow, you printed a copy for us?" I stammered, my voice registering a level of shock and awe at this unexpected session of "show and tell."

"Yeah," he said with a big laugh. "I figured out how to print these! It's my new toy! Do you want them?" he said playfully, extending the copies to Nate.

The truth was we were all a little repulsed by the pictures, reluctant to look at them. The last time we had viewed Nate's brain was in the neurosurgeon's office when the good doctor Wakefield tried repeatedly and unsuccessfully to measure the dreadful mass with his mouse on the computer screen.

"We'll do another MRI in three months and just keep on doing it," said Schneider into the silence that followed.

"For how long?" asked Norm.

"Every three months," replied Schneider.

"To be perfectly honest, part of the reason we're doing it every three months is that nobody has a lot of experience with these high-grade tectal gliomas," he said. "Yours is unusual—it's got a very good response now, but we've got to keep an eye on it."

We nodded.

Sensing our bewilderment, he launched into an explanation. "The truth is the majority of people we see here have very high-grade malignant brain tumors and we know exactly how they're going to behave. But this one . . . we can't predict it. We simply don't see responses like yours in high-grade malignant brain tumors.

"For instance, your scan from today," he said, leaning in, "I can't tell there was ever anything there. Whereas, in the vast majority of people we treat here, I can always tell where the tumor was—*always*! I can look at an MRI of the brain, flip up fast, and there it is.

"But this," he said after a short pause, "I always have to go back to your first slide, check that I have the correct birthdate and compare it—that's how improved it is. Pretty damn near printed off the wrong cut," he said, his laughter bubbling out, filling the room.

"What does that mean exactly?" I asked in a serious tone.

"What that means is that I can't *see* anything," he said emphatically, turning in my direction, his eyes bulging underneath those thick brows.

"With regular high-grade gliomas, I have no trouble finding the tumor bed at all, no matter how long ago they were treated, no matter how good the response was. In fact, we've been following a guy with a high-grade tumor for the last three years, and I can whip through the scans and easily find it, even though that person is not my patient. We see subtle changes in most people.

"But this," he said pointing to Nate's photocopies again, "this is *not* subtle. I've *never* seen a response this good."

Had we desired scientific proof that Nate's case was a miracle, these unsolicited pictures and this particular conversation provided solid evidence.

Someday, I thought, when we're further along the continuum of healing, I would pay Dr. Schneider a visit and interview him for the book that was shaping in my heart. I would ask him, human to human, about what he saw and how he felt. I would tell him how much we held on to his hope, and how grateful we were that he took the time to be real and honest, like we were his own. I would tell him he was a rare gift of a man, and an even rarer oncologist.

But I never got a chance. Dr. Schneider died two years later in 2014.


MY DAD PASSED AWAY on November 16, 2012, six weeks after Nate finished chemotherapy. The cancer in his body was more advanced than any of us had wanted to believe.

Five months later, in April 2013, Harry also died of cancer. And in the fall of that same year, our dear friend Warren was diagnosed with the disease. Cancer took his life in 2014.

I'm sure that in his last hours, my dad saw Jacob's heavenly staircase and a few fierce angels making their descent. We stood around his bed then, his body comatose, his breathing labored, except for one brief instant when his clear blue eyes opened saucer-wide, and he looked off into the distance.

"For goodness' sake!" he said with astonishment, his face brightening with wonder at the vision that held him captive. I had only ever heard him utter this phrase when he was face-to-face with something breathtaking, like when we drove through the Rocky Mountains on family camping trips when I was a kid.

No wonder the Anointing of the Sick, or last rites as it was traditionally called, is one of the seven sacraments for Catholic and Eastern Orthodox Christians. There is a thin veil that separates us from the heavens, gossamer thin when we accompany the soul at death. The living are not permitted a peek at the other side, but the dying can perceive it.

And just maybe, on occasion, that veil takes the shape of a ladder, a staircase, or even a crude-looking cross with a broken body—when heaven comes close enough for the living to see. Maybe Nate saw it, too, in the solitude of that radiation chamber.

Maybe the mercies granted for the living and the dying are not so different from each other—held together by the whisper of a word and the width of a monarch wing. Maybe the finish line is more transparent than we imagine.

Someday we will know. Until then, we must carry the mystery close to our hearts and remember its melody. If we listen closely, we can always hear it singing over us. *Mercy* is the refrain.

# Epilogue

I am convinced that the book of Jonah can best be read as God moving someone from a mere religious job, role, or career to an actual sense of personal call
of destiny.... It takes being "swallowed by a beast" and taken into a dark place
of nesting and nourishing that normally allows you to move to that deeper
place called personal vocation.

—RICHARD ROHR[1]

WHO ARE YOU NOW? That is the question that comes when grief is wrung
out. At first, I didn't hear it. But by June 2013, it began to surface, rumbled
around in my soul and called to me. Grief had made me fearless. Some of
the worst had happened and I had survived.

My dad had died. My mom, now eighty, was packing up her two-story
home 500 miles away, preparing to move her life to Winnipeg. My son, a
young adult cancer survivor, was making a recovery, taking tiny steps back
into the world. He had experimented with university, taking one course in
the winter and now dabbling with part-time—*very* part-time—work as a
landscaper.

There was also a new grandson. Laura and Jeff had welcomed their
first child, James, almost a year to the day we had received the news of Nate's
miracle scan. A bit of holy mischief? Absolutely.

I was a grandmother. To hold that little boy to my heart and smell his
new skin was an indescribable joy. His birth was a symbol of all that was
pure and new, life after death, a fresh page in our story. Resurrection.

But that question: *Who are you now?* It persisted. For two years, I
had been a primary caregiver. My work as a communications writer had

---

1. Rohr, *A Lever*, 85–86.

turned into a series of medical leaves, resulting in my resignation. I had willingly suspended my professional aspirations for the task of caregiving. I had no regrets.

But had I known what would be involved, I surely would have shriveled. That's the thing about this particular call: it comes on suddenly, like birth pangs, and requires you to learn on the fly.

Overnight, I had become an amateur pharmacist, doling out daily prescription drugs and researching side effects. I had become a nurse, administering Neupogen shots and monitoring reactions. I had become a dietician, planning meals to optimize protein intake and help rebuild healthy cells destroyed by chemotherapy.

I had become a psychologist, making sense of a world that was quickly coming apart and watching vigilantly for emotional responses that were uncharacteristic, disproportionate, or withdrawn and could signal a spiral into depression. I had become a spiritual director, watching with Nate for God's presence in his life and noticing how the story of God was unfolding in his story: on the lookout for mercy.

Ask anyone who's been a primary caregiver to a child with cancer and they'll tell you the journey is all-consuming. It is more than an interruption or a pause. It is a full stop, a period, a standstill in the flow of life.

I recoiled as I recalled the "great purge" that had taken place a few months earlier.

"Cleaned out the drug drawer in the kitchen this week," I wrote in my journal on April 25, "and purged our home of every reminder of pain and sickness. As if that were possible."

Yet it was a rite of passage for me, as it is for most primary caregivers of cancer patients.

Regardless of the outcome, life or death, the process of purging is the same.

The temozolomide bottle, worth $8,000, and another worth $4,000— discarded. I took a picture of the bottles with my phone. My gut turned when I saw "November 2011" on the sticker in the upper right-hand corner. That was a sickening season.

Among the clutter of pharmaceutical papers was a plethora of other blue bottles. How many anti-nausea meds did one person need? Ondansetron, along with breakthrough nausea pills, prescribed with every round—handfuls of the stuff—now destined for disposal. The blue kit that housed the costly Neupogen, with leftover vials of the white-cell maker. Gone.

There was a certain necessity, urgency even, that accompanied this task. It was sobering and not without tears, lots of them. Yes, I was thankful for a national healthcare program that covered the cost of treatment and for the formidable institution called CancerCare that provided the best of medical help.

But there was a particular satisfaction in ridding our home of these reminders. They were, after all, symbols of a way of life—and death. And these symbols were taking up physical and emotional room.

To purge is to make space for something new, even if that something is unknown.

WHO ARE YOU NOW? asked the voice within. Who are you now that the intensity of the crisis is over? Now that you are a grandmother? Now that you are a daughter with a mother moving close by? Will you continue down the path of caregiving, shapeshifting to fit the needs of those in your circle? Or is there something else in the making?

"What are the other dreams in your heart?" a friend asked.

"I have no clue," I said, surprised by the question.

Hadn't my son lived to see his twenty-third birthday? That was a dream. Shouldn't that be enough? Hadn't my daughter given birth to a child when conception had been a challenge? That was a dream. Shouldn't that be enough? It felt a little selfish to explore this question. It felt a little selfish to have any needs or dreams for myself at all.

In summer 2013, I began applying for jobs that had little to do with my training.

"I need an income stream," I told my friends. "Maybe ten hours a week, something that's not stressful, that gets me out and brings in some cash."

There was an opening in the healthcare system that fit my criteria. It wasn't exactly the kind of work that made use of my education, but it was employment, nonetheless.

Underneath my pragmatic approach, though, was a restlessness. How would the desire to write our sacred story find its way? Would my love of theology have any place in my vocational future?

Then in stepped another friend, my *anam cara*.

On my pilgrimage to Iona, I had picked up a book with a curious cover, titled with words from another tongue. It was called *Anam Cara*. Inside lived poetic language describing this forgotten Celtic craft.

In Gaelic, *anam cara* means "soul friend."

"In the early Celtic Church," explains author John O'Donohue, "a person who acted as a teacher, companion, or spiritual guide was called an *anam cara* . . . someone to whom you confessed, revealing the hidden intimacies of your life . . . [someone with whom] you could share your innermost self, your mind and your heart."[2]

So, when my friend Mary asked me that summer if I was interested in joining her for a two-year training program in the area of spiritual direction, I fumbled, fretted, and tossed out excuses. I couldn't possibly entertain the thought. There were bills to pay. How much was tuition? There was a stable but struggling young adult at home, a new grandbaby, a recently widowed mother. How could I possibly hold down a part-time job and study?

Mary was older than me by more than a decade. Her bobbed, silver hair, streaked with strands of gray, distinguished her as an elder. Her piercing gaze and thoughtful questions spoke of a hard-fought wisdom. It was what drew me to her in the first place. She possessed a quiet tenacity and rarely backed down.

"How can you be sure I'll be any good at this?" I asked Mary now, after exhausting my excuses.

"Because you've suffered," she said simply, her piercing gaze upon me.

Suffering as a prerequisite for the job? That was a new thought.

But in the wake of our conversation, I heard whispers of St. John of the Cross. "The dark night will leave its gifts, but you will not perceive it till the dawn."[3] Could this season signal the dawn, I wondered? Maybe. My heart trembled less, my skin wasn't as thin, my horizons had broadened.

So, what exactly might those gifts be, I mused?

"There will always be a situation in our lives that we cannot fix, control, explain, change, or even understand," says Richard Rohr, a kind of falling, a necessary suffering that vaults us into the second half of life, where meaning and mystery hold us together.[4]

For Jesus and his followers, the necessary suffering, the absurd stumbling stone, was the crucifixion.

For me, the necessary suffering was the presence of a lethal tumor in my son. Thrust into the second half of life, I was learning to listen for the deeper voice of God and it sounded an "awful lot like the voices of risk, of trust, of surrender of soul, of 'common sense,' of destiny, of love."[5]

Oddly enough, this falling opened my soul wide to God as Mystery and created a largeness inside. Gone was my sense of entitlement—that life owed me years, that time was mine. Gone were expired expectations of what I should do or who I thought I should be. Gone was the need for

---

2. O'Donohue, *Anam Cara*, 35.

3. May, *The Dark Night of the Soul*, 3.

4. Rohr, *Falling Upward*, 68.

5. Rohr, *Falling Upward*, 48.

approval that had cluttered many of my earlier decisions—to be and do what others expected.

Suffering had carved out a crater-sized hole, purging me of the things I thought I had wanted and thought I knew. In their place was a capacity to live in the present and be more perceptive to mercy. It felt an awful lot like freedom "to join the dance of life in fullness without having a clue about what the steps are."[6]

The energy to respond to the call came quietly and rose steadily over the course of that summer. It culminated in a midnight epiphany.

I was at the lake on a sultry August night, tossing and turning in my bed. My thoughts and emotions were a jumbled mess when I heard it. Just beyond the open window. The sound of waves lapping on the shore. An oceanic sound heard the world over, the earth's metronome.

How had I failed to hear this lovely sound before? Had the waves kept me company the whole time? For an entire minute, I breathed in wave-time, in sync with the soothing center at the heart of creation.

*Inhale. Exhale.*

I continued to breathe this way for another minute. And then another. A calm settled over me and grace slipped in.

And I was reminded, again, that a being far bigger than I was in charge of the universe. It may not have been a word like *Gotcha* that I received that night. But it was every bit as revolutionary, this ancient breath of God, inviting me in.

Suddenly, my need to resolve things, my demand for answers, my obsessive-compulsive tangents, my what ifs, relaxed against this cosmic heartbeat, this rhythmic Divine, lapping faith, hope, and love onto the shores of my life.

"Listen to the waves," God seemed to be saying. "Listen for the frequency that exists underneath the chatter of your mind. There you will find me and connect with my soothing center at the heart of creation."

And this was mercy.

Spiritual direction, the vocation Mary had invited me to consider, is that simple and that complex. It's hard work.

I took one step, then another.

I said "yes" to the part-time job. I also applied for the training program in spiritual direction. Maybe I would become an *anam cara*, a spiritual director, maybe I wouldn't.

But one thing was certain: I would follow this leading, if only as an avenue to process my experience of the dark night and to live more deeply

6. May, *The Dark Night of the Soul*, 133.

from it. My soul was hungry for meaning. If, at some point, I could help others experience God in the dark and find a way forward, so be it.

There were still questions floating in my consciousness. How would I balance the new job? How would my mom manage her move? How would I take care of the daily demands of food preparation and diet for my son? How would Nate manage without me twenty-four seven? But these questions no longer felt paralyzing.

That fall, after looking at the syllabus and ordering the books, I smiled and thought, "I can't *not* go ahead with this coursework."

Inside, I felt a sneaky little sparkle of pure delight—like being on an expansive beach of soft sand and hearing a playful invitation, "Take off your shoes and run!" *How good it would feel to run.*

Had you told me any of this before the mid-August divide in 2011, how dying a thousand deaths would resurrect a new kind of faith, hope, and love in me, I would have turned and run in the opposite direction.

Had you told me that after his devastating cancer diagnosis and drastic treatment, Nate would claw and scrape his way through university and graduate with his business degree at twenty-eight, I might have hugged you tight and thought you crazy.

Had you whispered that, just a year later, Nate would move out and marry his soul mate, Diana, I surely would have laughed out loud in disbelief.

How are all these things possible? How is it possible to live in the shadow of death and grieve a child, a parent, a friend, a doctor—any loved one—yet still hold on to hope?

Because the shape of mercy is never predictable—or safe, for that matter. Because his good is always immeasurably more than we can ask or imagine. Because his name is Mercy.

One thing is certain. The poster in the hallway of the fifth-floor step-down unit was indeed true. A brain tumor really does change everything.

# Bibliography

Alexander, Irene, et al. "Liminal Space and Transitions in the Journey." *Conversations Journal,* vol. 2:2 (Fall, 2004) 18–23.

Barton, Ruth Haley. "The Journey from Spiritual Blindness to Spiritual Sight." *Conversations Journal,* vol. 10.2 (Fall/Winter, 2012) 77–81.

Berry, Wendell. *The Selected Poems of Wendell Berry.* Berkeley: Counterpoint, 1998.

Brain Tumour Foundation of Canada. *Brain Tumour Patient Resource Handbook Adult Version.* London Ontario: Brain Tumour Foundation of Canada, 2009.

Brain Tumour Foundation of Canada. "Facts About Brain Tumours." https://www. braintumour.ca/facing-a-brain-tumour/facts-about-brain-tumours.

Brother Lawrence of the Resurrection. *The Practice of the Presence of God.* New York: Doubleday, 1977.

Brueggemann, Walter. *A Way Other Than Our Own: Devotions for Lent.* Louisville: Westminster John Knox, 2017. Kindle.

Buechner, Frederick. *Telling Secrets: A Memoir.* New York: HarperCollins, 1991. Kindle.

Canadian Partnership Against Cancer. "Adolescents & Young Adults with Cancer in Canada." https://s22457.pcdn.co/wp-content/uploads/2019/01/Adolescents-and-young-adults-with-cancer-EN.pdf.

Chittister, Joan D. *Scarred by Struggle, Transformed by Hope.* Grand Rapids: Eerdmans, 2003.

Chittister, Joan, and Rowan Williams. *Uncommon Gratitude: Alleluia for All That Is.* Collegeville: Liturgical, 2010.

Diadochus of Photiki. "On Spiritual Knowledge and Discrimination: One Hundred Texts." In *The Philokalia,* vol. 1, compiled by St. Nikodimos of the Holy Mountain and St. Makarios of Corinth, trans., eds., G.E.H. Palmer, Philip Sherrard and Kallistos Ware. 251–96. London: Faber and Faber, 1979. http://holybooks. lichtenbergpress.netdna-cdn.com/wp-content/uploads/Philokalia.pdf.

Government of Canada. "End-of-life care." https://www.canada.ca/en/services/benefits /ei/caregiving.html.

Griffin, Emilie. *Wonderful and Dark Is This Road: Discovering the Mystic Path.* Brewster: Paraclete, 2004.

Kalanithi, Paul. *When Breath Becomes Air.* New York: Random House, 2016. Kindle.

Katz, Anne. *This Should Not Be Happening: Young Adults with Cancer.* Pittsburgh: Hygiea Media, 2014.

Kelley, Thomas R. *A Testament of Devotion.* New York: Harper & Row, 1941.

Laird, Martin. *Into the Silent Land: A Guide to the Christian Practice of Contemplation.* New York: Oxford University Press, 2006.

MacNutt, Francis. *Healing.* Notre Dame: Ave Maria Press, 1974.

May, Gerald G. *The Dark Night of the Soul: A Psychiatrist Explores the Connection Between Darkness and Spiritual Growth.* New York: HarperCollins, 2004.

———. *The Wisdom of the Wilderness: Experiencing the Healing Power of Nature.* New York: HarperCollins, 2006. Kindle.

Newell, Philip J. *Listening for the Heartbeat of God: A Celtic Spirituality.* New York: Paulist, 1997.

Norris, Kathleen. *Amazing Grace: A Vocabulary of Faith.* New York: Riverhead, 1998.

———. "Fourth Monday of Advent." In *God With Us: Rediscovering the Meaning of Christmas,* edited by Greg Pennoyer and Gregory Wolfe, 105–06. Brewster: Paraclete, 2007.

Nouwen, Henri J. M. *Life of the Beloved: Spiritual Living in a Secular World.* New York: Crossroad, 1992.

———. *The Way of the Heart: Desert Spirituality and Contemporary Ministry.* New York: HarperCollins, 1991.

O'Donohue, John. *Anam Cara: Spiritual Wisdom from the Celtic World.* London: Bantam, 1997.

———. *To Bless the Space Between Us: A Book of Blessings.* New York: Convergent, 2008.

Palmer, Parker J. *Let Your Life Speak: Listening for the Voice of Vocation.* San Francisco: Jossey-Bass, 2000.

Peterson, Eugene H. *Christ Plays in Ten Thousand Places: A Conversation in Spiritual Theology.* Grand Rapids: Eerdmans, 2005.

Phillips, Susan S. *Candlelight: Illuminating the Art of Spiritual Direction.* Harrisburg: Morehouse, 2008. Kindle.

Pope Francis. *The Name of God is Mercy.* New York: Random House, 2016.

Reuter, Orit. "Who cares for the caregiver? How are the needs of primary malignant brain tumour patients met through structured neuro-oncology programs in Canadian Centres?" https://mspace.lib.umanitoba.ca/bitstream/handle/1993/4983/reuter_orit.pdf?sequence=1.

Rohr, Richard. *Falling Upward: A Spirituality for the Two Halves of Life.* San Francisco: Jossey-Bass, 2011.

———. *Immortal Diamond: The Search for Our True Self.* San Francisco: Jossey-Bass, 2013.

———. *A Lever and a Place to Stand: The Contemplative Stance, the Active Prayer.* Mahwah: HiddenSpring, 2011.

———. *The Naked Now: Learning to See as the Mystics See.* New York: Crossroad, 2009.

———. "True Conversion Never Stops." https://cac.org/true-conversion-never-stops-2017-02-10/.

Rolf, Veronica Mary. *Julian of Norwich.* Downers Grove: InterVarsity, 2018.

Schmemann, Alexander. *Great Lent: Journey to Pascha.* New York: St. Vladimir's Seminary Press, 1969.

Shaw, Luci. *Accompanied by Angels: Poems of the Incarnation.* Grand Rapids: Eerdmans, 2006.

Silf, Margaret. *Born to Fly: A Handbook for Butterflies-in-Waiting.* London: Darton, Longman and Todd, 2017.

———. Forward to *Inheriting Paradise: Meditations on Gardening*, by Vigen Guroian, iv. Grand Rapids: Eerdmans, 1999.

St. John of the Cross. *The Collected Works of St. John of the Cross*. Translated by Kieran Kavanaugh and Otilio Rodriguez. Washington: ICS, 2017.

Taylor, Barbara Brown. *Learning to Walk in the Dark*. New York: HarperCollins, 2014. Kindle.

Tickle, Phyllis. *The Divine Hours: Prayers for Summertime*. New York: Doubleday, 2000.

Trible, Phyllis. *God and the Rhetoric of Sexuality*. Philadelphia: Fortress, 1986.

Walsh, James, ed. *The Cloud of Unknowing*. The Classics of Western Spirituality. Mahwah: Paulist, 1981.

Webber, Robert E. *Evangelicals on the Canterbury Trail: Why Evangelicals are Attracted to the Liturgical Church*. New York: Morehouse, 1985.

Wright, N. T. *Simply Christian: Why Christianity Makes Sense*. New York: HarperCollins, 2006.

Young Adult Cancer Canada. "Our History." https://www.youngadultcancer.ca/history/.

Made in United States
Troutdale, OR
08/10/2023

11967681R00096